Varṇa Śikṣā: The Qualities, Colors, Genders and Devatās of the Letters of the Sanskrit Alphabet

translated by
Peter F. Freund

Golden Meteor Press—Fairfield, Iowa

ISBN-10: 151681360X
ISBN-13: 978-1516813605

Printed by Golden Meteor Press, Fairfield, Iowa, U.S.A., 2015

Acknowledgements:

Thanks to the Mysore Oriental Manuscript Library for making photographs of the Varṇa Śikṣā manuscript available. Thanks also to team members Vivek Vaidyanathan and Detlef Eichler, without whose help this text would not have come to light.

Table of Contents

1. The Sanskrit Alphabet IV
2. Prolog: The Vedas and Vedic Literature XI
3. Preface: The Significance of Śikṣā, the ancient Vedic Science of Speech 1
4. Overview 5
   A. Introduction to Varṇa Śikṣā 5
   B. Section 1 of Varṇa Śikṣā: Gender of the letters of the alphabet 11
   C. Section 2: Qualities of Sattva, Rajas and Tamas of letters of the alphabet 14
   D. Section 3: The Devatā, Color, and Fruit (*Phalaśruti*) of each letter 16
   E. The seer of Varṇa Śikṣā 25
   F. The unique contribution of Varṇa Śikṣā 28
   G. The relationship of name and form in Varṇa Śikṣā 31
5. English translation of Varṇa Śikṣā 39
6. The Devatās of Varṇa Śikṣā 55
7. Summary of Characteristics of the Letters 87
8. Sanskrit text of Varṇa Śikṣā with transliteration 91
9. Sanskrit text of Varṇa Śikṣā large type 101
10. Appendix: A Vision of the Complete Science of Śikṣā 115
11. Epilog by Maharishi Mahesh Yogi 125
12. Index 133

50 LETTERS OF THE SANSKRIT ALPHABET

अ a	आ ā	इ i	ई ī	उ u
ऊ ū	ऋ ṛ	ॠ ṝ	ऌ lṛ	ॡ lṝ
ए e	ऐ ai	ओ o	औ au	
अं aṁ	अः aḥ			
क ka	ख kha	ग ga	घ gha	ङ ṅa
च ca	छ cha	ज ja	झ jha	ञ ña
ट ṭa	ठ ṭha	ड ḍa	ढ ḍha	ण ṇa
त ta	थ tha	द da	ध dha	न na
प pa	फ pha	ब ba	भ bha	म ma
य ya	र ra	ल la	व va	
श śa	ष ṣa	स sa	ह ha	ळ ḷa

अ a

gender: masc.
quality: rajas
color: red
devatā: All Devatās

आ ā

gender: fem.
quality: sattva
color: white
devatā: Parāśakti

इ i

gender: masc.
quality: tamas
color: black
devatā: Viṣṇu

ई ī

gender: fem.
quality: rajas
color: yellow
devatā: Māyā Śakti

उ u

gender: masc.
quality: tamas
color: black
devatā: Vāstu

ऊ ū

gender: fem.
quality: tamas
color: black
devatā: Bhūmi

ऋ ṛ

gender: neuter
quality: rajas
color: yellow
devatā: Brahman

ॠ ṝ

gender: neuter
quality: rajas
color: yellow
devatā: Śikhaṇḍirūpa

ऌ

lṛ

gender: neuter
quality: rajas
color: red
devatā: Aśvin Nāsatya

ॡ

lṝ

gender: neuter
quality: rajas
color: red
devatā: Aśvin Dasra

ए

e

granting siddhis

gender: masc.
quality: rajas
color: yellow
devatā: Vīrabhadra

ऐ

ai

gender: fem.
quality: sattva
color: white
devatā: Vāgbhava

ओ

o

bestowing fruit

gender: masc.
quality: sattva
color: white (Jyoti)
devatā: Īśvara

औ

au

success in all things

gender: fem.
quality: sattva
color: white
devatā: Ādiśakti

अं

aṁ

gender: masc.
quality: rajas
color: red
devatā: Maheśa

अः

aḥ

gender: fem.
quality: rajas
color: red
devatā: Kālarudra

क ka

gender: masc.
quality: rajas
color: yellow
devatā: Prajāpati

bestowing rain

ख kha

gender: fem.
quality: sattva
color: white
devatā: Jāhnavī

destroying sin

ग ga

gender: masc.
quality: rajas
color: red
devatā: Gaṇapati

eliminating obstacles

घ gha

gender: fem.
quality: sattva
color: white
devatā: Bhairava

destroying enemies

ङ ṅa

gender: neuter
quality: tamas
color: black
devatā: Kāla

overcoming death

च ca

gender: masc.
quality: tamas
color: black
devatā: Caṇḍarudra

छ cha

gender: fem.
quality: tamas
color: black
devatā: Bhadrakālī

bringing fame

ज ja

gender: masc.
quality: rajas
color: red
devatā: (Indra) Jambhahā

bringing victory

झ

jha

gender: fem.
quality: tamas
color:red-blk.
devatā:
Ardhanārīśa

ञ

ña

gender: neuter
quality: rajas
color: yellow
devatā:
Sarpadevatā

ट

ṭa

gender: masc.
quality: rajas
color: red
devatā:
Bhṛṅgīśa

ठ

ṭha

gender: fem.
quality: sattva
color: white
devatā: Candra
(Moon)

ड

ḍa

gender: masc.
quality: rajas
color: yellow
devatā:
Ekanetra

ढ

destroying
death

ḍha

gender: fem.
quality: tamas
color: blue
devatā:
Yama

ण

achieving
the goal

ṇa

gender: neuter
quality: rajas
color: red
devatā:
Nandi

त

ta

gender: masc.
quality: sattva
color: white
devatā: Vāstu
Devatā

थ tha

gender: fem.
quality: sattva
color: white
devatā: Brahman

द da

granting success

gender: masc.
quality: tamas
color: black
devatā: Durgā

ध dha

achieving the goal

gender: fem.
quality: rajas
color: yellow
devatā: Dhanada

न na

destroying sin

gender: neuter
quality: sattva
color: crystal
devatā: Sāvitrī

प pa

perfection in rain

gender: masc.
quality: sattva
color: white
devatā: Parjanya

फ pha

destroying sin

gender: fem.
quality: sattva
color: white
devatā: Paśupati

ब ba

granting success

gender: masc.
quality: rajas
color: yellow
devatā: Trimūrti

भ bha

bestowing fortune

gender: fem.
quality: rajas
color: red
devatā: Bhārgava

म ma

gender: neuter
quality: tamas
color: black
devatā: Madana

bestowing all fruits

य ya

gender: neuter
quality: tamas
color: black
devatā: Vāyu

destroying enemies

र ra

gender: neuter
quality: rajas
color: red
devatā: Vahni Devatā

ल la

gender: neuter
quality: rajas
color: yellow
devatā: Pṛthivī

supporting procurement

व va

gender: neuter
quality: sattva
color: white
devatā: Varuṇa

destroying boundaries

श śa

gender: fem.
quality: rajas
color: gold
devatā: Lakṣmī

ष ṣa

gender: masc.
quality: rajas
color: red
devatā: Dvādaśātmā

bestowing victory

स sa

gender: fem.
quality: rajas
color: red
devatā: Śakti

creating stability

ह

ha

gender: neuter
quality: sattva
color: white
devatā: Śiva

bestowing 8 siddhis

ळ

ḷa

gender: neuter
quality: rajas
color: red
devatā: Ātmā

granting all success

THE VEDAS AND VEDIC LITERATURE

The Vedas are the eternal uncreated blueprint of total natural law at the basis of creation. The unifying foundation of order and intelligence recognized by modern physics as the Unified Field of All the Laws of Nature was known to the ancient sages of the Vedic Tradition of India as the field of Absolute Being, Brahman, characterized as Sat-Cit-Ānanda, "eternal bliss consciousness." It is unmanifest Truth having the structure of pure knowledge, lively with the Self-referral impulses of Total Natural Law. The impulses of Natural Law that make up the structure of pure knowledge at the basis of the whole universe are the ṛcas of the Veda and Vedic Literature—cognitions of eternal truths that are valid for all mankind at all times and all places.

> Veda is the structure and function of pure knowledge. It encompasses the whole range of science and technology; it is theory and practice at the same time; it is the structure of total knowledge—Saṁhitā of Ṛsi, Devatā, Chandas—the togetherness (Saṁhitā) of the observer (Ṛsi), process of

> observation (Devatā) and object of observation (Chandas).
>
> Therefore, 'Vedic' includes the whole path of knowledge from the knower to the known—the whole field of subjectivity, objectivity, and their relationship; the whole field of life, unmanifest and manifest; the whole field of 'Being' and 'Becoming'; the whole range of knowledge from its source to its goal—the eternal source, course and goal of all knowledge.[1]

His Holiness Maharishi Mahesh Yogi has assembled and organized the scattered texts of Vedic Literature into a complete and perfect science of life. Maharishi Vedic Science is comprised of 40 branches: Four Vedas and six groups of six branches. (See diagram, page 38). These sciences systematically encompass the whole range of natural law from point to infinity.

With this foundation of the vision of total knowledge of Natural Law which Maharishi has unfolded for us in his presentation of the 40 branches of Vedic Science, now in this series of monographs, we will be examining in depth the texts of one of these 40 branches, Śikṣā, the first of the Vedāṅga loop. We begin with Maharishi's synopsis of the unique role of Śikṣā in the field of Vedic Literature.

---

1 Maharishi Mahesh Yogi, *Vedic Knowledge for Everyone: Maharishi Vedic University: Introduction*, Maharishi Vedic University Press, Holland: 1994, p.5.

His Holiness Maharishi Mahesh Yogi

Śikṣā:

Śikṣā is one of the structuring dynamics of Ṛk Veda. It highlights the quality of EXPRESSION involved in structuring Ṛk Veda.

With reference to consciousness, Śikṣā comprises the specific sets of Laws of Nature that are engaged in promoting the quality of Ṛṣi within Saṁhitā, providing a structure to the eternally silent, self-referral, self-sufficient, fully awake state of consciousness, which is intimately personal to everyone.

Maharishi Mahesh Yogi, *Vedic Knowledge for Everyone: Maharishi Vedic University Introduction*, Maharishi Vedic University Press: Holland, 1994, pp. 86-87.

Professor Tony Nader, MD, PhD

Śikṣā represents the quality of expression of self-referral consciousness with reference to Ṛṣi within the nature of Saṁhitā. There are 36 main books of Śikṣā. In the physiology, Śikṣā is represented by the structures that compute and express the internal aspects of the physiology, such as its biochemical constituents, temperature, pressure, etc. (the expressions of the autonomic nervous system). These expressions are the components that maintain the homeostatic balance of the internal milieu, and are channelled via the autonomic ganglia. There are 36 on each side of the spinal cord, corresponding to the 36 books of Śikṣā.

Professor Tony Nader, MD, PhD,
Human Physiology: Expression of Veda and the Vedic Literature: Modern Science and Ancient Vedic Science Discover the Fabrics of Immortality in the Human Physiology,
Maharishi Vedic University Press: Holland, 2000, pp. 100-101.

The Vedic Science of Speech

The Ṛg Veda, the most ancient record of human experience, declares "Ṛco akṣare." (I.164.39) The ṛcas, the verses of the Veda, exist in the collapse, "kṣara," of the sound "a." As the completely unrestricted full-bodied sound of the fully open throat and mouth, "a," collapses as the throat chokes down to create the non-moving silent point of the letter "ka," there is the systematic step by step annihilation of the infinite unbounded potential for expression in speech contained in the sound "a." The seers of the Vedas, examining closely the collapse of "a" into "ka," cognized sequential stages of this move of sound into silence. The dynamism of the completely open organ of speech articulates all the pure Svaras, the pure vowel sounds, as it comes to a stop in the unmoving infinitesimal point of "ka." The seers identified eight stages of dynamism collapsing to silence, eight somersaults of the contracting reverberation of "a" as "a" becomes "i" then "u" and "ṛ" and "lṛ" and "e" and "o" and lastly the nasal vowel "aṁ" as the fully open "a" becomes fully closed "ka." These eight somersaults of "a" trace out the path of expression from unmanifest abstract potentiality of all possibilities to the complete inertia of the fully articulated manifest point value of silence in "ka." The somersaults flow sequentially through all the eight elements of Nature, called Prakṛtis: Ego, intellect, mind, space, air, fire, water and earth. These eight Prakṛtis encompass the whole range of Natural Law. Infinite unbounded pure abstract Natural Law creates manifest creation through these eight stages, eight somersaults contained in the simple flow of speech from "a" to "ka."

This is the field of Śikṣā, the Vedic science of phonology, the science of speech. In the range between the dynamism of "a" and the silence of "ka" the total knowledge and organizing power of Natural Law on every level of creation—all the ṛcas of the Veda—is contained. Everything that there is to experience in all the possible worlds of experience, and everything there is to know in all the worlds of the manifest and the unmanifest, and all the potential for action, for organizing power, everything is contained there in the collapse of "a" to "ka"—it is the fundamental unit of speech, and the ultimate paradigm of Total Natural Law. The Vedic science of speech contains everything that one needs for complete illumination of the reality of life, and total unfoldment of the latent infinite potential of every human being. Śikṣā has everything that one needs for complete enlightenment, for raising individual awareness to the highest state of consciousness, the level of unbounded comprehension of the total field of Natural Law in Brahman Consciousness.

A. Introduction to Varṇa Śikṣa

The full sound of the letter "a", throat and mouth open, collapsing and coming to a point in the letter "ka," throat fully closed and silent, is called by Maharishi Mahesh Yogi[1] the "*kṣara*" or collapse, of "a." The *kṣara* of "a", or "*a-kṣara*" is the paradigm for the creation of all the letters of the alphabet. The word "*Akṣara*" means "letter,"and it also means, "imperishable," in Sanskrit.

अक्षर

akṣara = a + kṣara
a: the letter "a"
kṣara: from root √ kṣar
√ kṣar: to melt away, wane, perish,
to fall or slip from, be deprived of

a-kṣara: The collapse of infinity, "a,"
into its own point, "ka."

In the collapse of "a" to "ka," all the letters of the alphabet are generated. In the collapse of "a" to "ka," in what are called the eight somersaults of "a," all the eight elements of creation, called *Prakṛtis* are fully elaborated and explored, and thereby all the worlds, all knowledge, all organizing power, is fully unfolded in those eight somersaults.

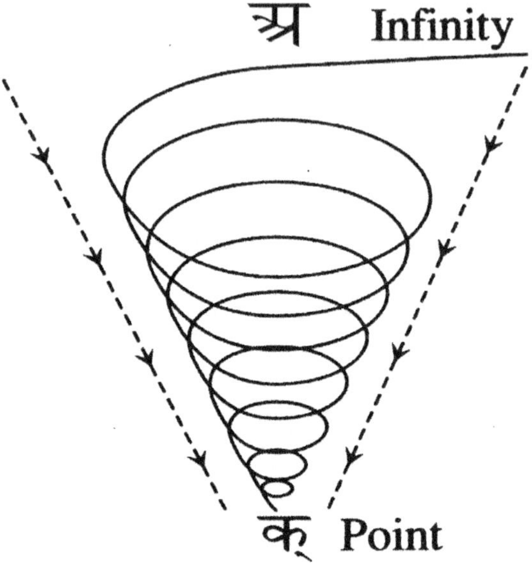

The collapse of infinity, "a" to its own point, "ka."
Everything is contained there: "a to k," "ak" is the first syllable of the Ṛg Veda, the seed of total knowledge, and the source, course and goal of the study of phonology, the science of sound, known as *Śikṣā*. *Śikṣā*, the study of expression in speech, opens the door to total knowledge of life, total knowledge of reality.

The potential of every human being is infinite, and that infinity is lively in every word and every letter that a person speaks. Realization of the Self means realization of the infinite unbounded potential of one's own inner nature. The knowledge of the alphabet, the knowledge of how to pronounce sounds properly provided by the Vedic science of Śikṣā, is the gateway to complete unfoldment of the unbounded potential for supreme knowledge and infinite organizing power latent in every human being.

Śikṣā, Vedic phonology, is a wide ranging field with more than a hundred different texts. But in its most basic and fundamental incarnations, it is the study of the Sanskrit alphabet. Many important Śikṣā texts explicitly explore the letters of the alphabet. There are many which enumerate and categorize the different speech sounds, such as Gautama Śikṣā, which identifies 25 full contact consonants, four semi-vowels, four sibilants, and four yamas. Some Śikṣā texts, such as Āpiśali Śikṣā and Ātreya Śikṣā list the letters of the alphabet at the start of their discussion of the details of pronunciation and the mechanics of expression.

ह्रस्वदीर्घप्लुतावर्णौवर्णौवर्णा ऋ ॠ ऌ च २
एदैदोदौदिति ज्ञेयाः षोडशेहादिताः स्वराः
कखौ गघौ ङचछजा झञौ टठडढा णतौ ३
थदौ धनौ पफबभा मः स्पर्शाः पञ्चविंशतिः
यरौ लवौ चतस्रोऽन्तस्थाश्चः कशषसः पहाः ४

षड्रूष्मानो विसर्गोऽनुस्वारो ळो नास्यपञ्चकम्
इत्येते याजुषा वर्णा एकोनाःषष्टिरीरिताः ५
hrasva-dīrgha-pluta-a-varṇa-i-varṇa-u-varṇa ṛ ṝ lṛ ca 2
ed-aid-od-aud-iti jñeyāḥ ṣoḍaśa-iha-āditāḥ svarāḥ
kakhau gaghau ṅacachajā jhañau ṭaṭhaḍaḍhā ṇatau 3
thadau dhanau paphababhā maḥ sparśāḥ pañca-viṁśatiḥ
yarau lavau catasro'ntasthāś caḥkaśaṣasaḥpahāḥ 4
ṣaḍūṣmāno visargo'nusvāro ḷo nāsya pañcakam
ityete yājuṣo varṇā ekonāḥ ṣaṣṭirīritāḥ 5

59 letters of Yajur Veda described by Ātreya Śikṣā[2]

Finally, there is one Śikṣā that devotes itself entirely to enumerating and describing the 50 basic speech sounds of the Sanskrit language. That is Varṇa Śikṣā, a newly discovered and unexpected find, hidden in a bundle of more than 100 Telugu-script palm leaves from Mysore, India.

The speciality of Sanskrit language is that the relationship between the sound and its corresponding form or object, is not a symbolic relationship: It is not a man-made association between groups of sounds and qualities of a form: There is claimed to be an eternal relationship between the sound of the Sanskrit word and its corresponding form. Jaimini, author of the fifth system of Indian philosophy, *Karma Mīmāṁsā,* explains:

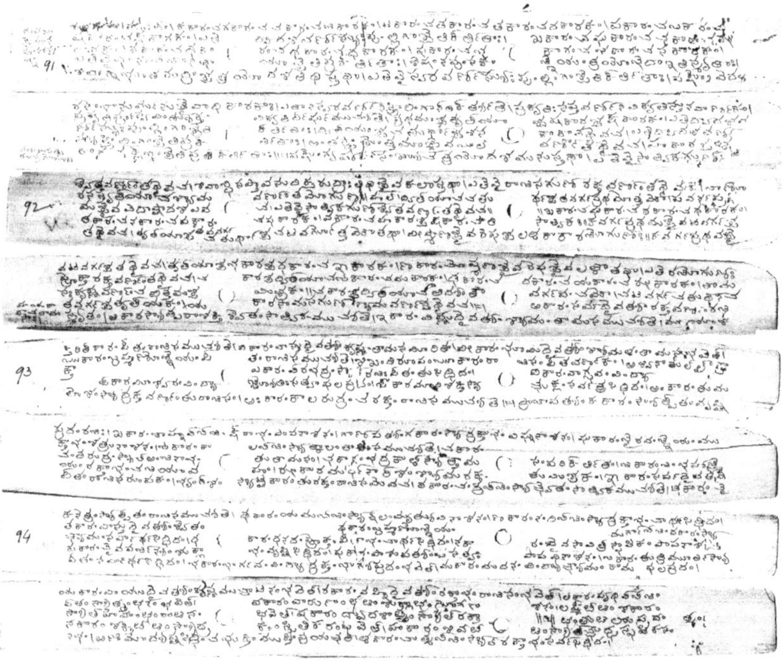

Complete Manuscript of Varṇa Śikṣā

औत्पत्तिकस्तु शब्दस्यार्थेन सम्बन्धस्तस्य

ज्ञानमुपदेशोऽव्यतिरेकश्चार्थेऽनुपलब्धे

तत्प्रमाणं बादरायणस्यानपेक्षत्वात् ५

"Certainly there is eternal connection between the word and its meaning; its knowledge is intrinsic to the field of consciousness. It is never erroneous in matters invisible; it is authoritative in the opinion of Bādarāyaṇa by reason of its not depending on others."

I.1.5 *Karma Mīmāṁsā Sūtra* of Jaimini[3]

This means that the sound has the same qualities as the form at each stage of its development and manifestation; sound and form both follow the same sequential steps of evolution of expression. Therefore one can experience the truth of the Vedic sounds on the level of consciousness, the same in any age.

In the Vedic system of education, the Vedic system of gaining knowledge, one learns how to pronounce the Vedic sounds correctly, and then one refines one's individual nervous system through the practice of Yoga—that means, in our generation, through the Transcendental Meditation® and T.M.-Sidhi® program—until one gains a level of pure consciousness described by Patanjali as *Ritaṁ Bharā Pragyā*, that level of consciousness which only supports Truth.

ऋतम्भरा तत्र प्रज्ञा ४८
Ṛtam bharā tatra prajñā
I.48, Patañjali Yoga Sūtra[4]

On that level of consciousness, the form of the corresponding sound will show up as on a television screen in full clarity. So in Vedic education, noone bothers about the meaning; the meaning of the Vedic words isn't taught. What is taught is the technology for unfolding the meaning in one's own consciousness, through the eternal correspondence of name and form. The result of this approach of Vedic Education is that total knowledge can be unfolded in one's awareness in a short time. The example is given of Rāma, the hero of the Rāmāyaṇa, who gained total knowledge of life without being subjected to a long and tedious educational process:

> अल्पकाल विद्या सब आई
>
> Alpakāl vidyā sab āī
>
> Total Knowledge gained in a short time.
>
> —Rāma Carita Mānasa,
> Bāl Kāṇḍa 203.2

B. Section 1 of Varṇa Śikṣā: Gender of the Letters of the Alphabet

Let's look more closely at this vision of ideal education, education which consists merely in repeating the sounds of Vedic speech. We start from the one unbounded wholeness of consciousness, flat, pure oneness of pure consciousness, Samādhi, transcendental consciousness, silence, what is called the *Pātañjali kaivalya.*

Now, after long experience of that silence, some weeks or months or years on the Invincible America Assembly (an ongoing course for advanced practitioners of the T.M.® and T.M.-Sidhi® program, in Fairfield, Iowa, U.S.A.), that pure silence starts to have some liveliness within it.[5] It starts to be not so flat, but textured, it has within it at first some few sparks, here and there, and then eventually the one flat ocean is seen to be made of innumerable points of dynamism, fluctuation, motion, and light everywhere. It is no longer just flat, but it has become the embodiment of infinite dynamism, innumerable points of lively intelligence.

Now, as Maharishi described in a lecture entitled, "The Unmanifest Home of Creative Intelligence," (1976)[6] each point is a point of consciousness. Within that wholeness of lively dynamic pure wakefulness, a separation develops, as if a line is created within the one unbounded ocean, and two sides, two qualities of consciousness are located, the knower, and the known. Consciousness creates its own object within itself. Within the wholeness of consciousness, there is a relationship between the knower and the known, between Purusha, the silent witness, and Prakriti, the dynamism of organizing power—but all within the unmanifest. In this stage of consciousness knowing itself, some of the impulses take on the role of the seer, or witness, or "knower," and others of the impulses take on the role of the seen, or "known," while some take up the position of the neutral point between the two sides, accentuating the division into two. Yet all of these are impulses.

The seer of Varṇa Śikṣā calls these three groups masculine, feminine, and neuter. The consonants and vowels of the Sanskrit alphabet are classified in this way, as either masculine, feminine or neuter. This means that the knowledge of the fundamental relationship between the knower and the known within the structure of pure consciousness, pure knowledge, is made manifest in terms of the specific gender assigned to each letter. This is a very precious knowledge of the inherent qualities of the Vedic sounds which go to make up the forms and phenomena of all of relative creation.

Masculine, Feminine and Neuter letters of the Sanskrit Alphabet

Masculine letters:	a, i, u, e, o, aṁ, ka, ga, ca, ja, ṭa, ḍa, ta, da, pa, ba, ṣa, kṣa
Feminine letters:	ā, ī, ū, ai, au, aḥ, kha, gha, cha, jha, ṭha, ḍha, tha, dha, pha, bha, śa, sa
Neuter letters:	ṛ, ṝ, lṛ, ya, ra, la, va, ṅa, ña, ṇa, na, ma, ha, ḷa

C. Section 2 of Varṇa Śikṣā: Qualities of Sattva, Rajas and Tamas of Letters of the Alphabet

Having shown this relationship between the knower and the known, arising within the one unbounded ocean of pure consciousness, the seer of the Varṇa Śikṣā takes the analysis one step further, revealing yet another fundamental classification of impulses of natural law at the basis of creation. Among the impulses within the ocean of consciousness, there are impulses which are completely devoted to maintaining the integrity of the wholeness, upholding the oneness of the unbounded ocean of consciousness. There is yet another class of impulses, within the fabrics of the Absolute, which, even though not having any connection with anything outside of wholeness, nevertheless, has a tendency for diversification within the structure of wholeness: The 8 Vasus, the 11 Rudras created out of the wholeness of the one Śiva, the 15 steps or Tithis in the flow from New Moon to Full Moon, and the 16 Kalās in the Vedic Maṇḍala representing the 8 somersaults from fullness into the gap, and then 8 somersaults back out into fullness, these are all expressions of a tendency of diversification, without actually entering into diversity. So we have two categories, upholding the integration and oneness of the field, and creating a tendency for diversification within the structure of wholeness. Maharishi called these two kinds of impulses within the one unbounded ocean of Self-referral consciousness, "Pu"-impulses" and "Pra"-impulses, in response to a question from Nobel laureate Dr. Brian Josephson.[7] The seer of Varṇa Śikṣā calls these impulses which uphold unity and oneness, sattvic impulses, sattvic letters and they are white in color. Those which have some little tendency to diversification within the structure of wholeness he calls rajasic, and they are red in color. Those letters which connect sattva and rajas together and create a dynamic flow, are called tamasic, and these have a black color. This is a second broad categorization of the letters of the Sanskrit alphabet. The division of the letters of the alphabet into these three categories gives deep insight into the mechanics of creation of the form from the sound. It exposes the delicate structure of relationship between impulses in the unmanifest.

Sattvic, Rajasic, and Tamasic letters of the Sanskrit Alphabet

Sattvic letters:	ā, ai, o, au, kha, gha, ṭha, ta, tha, na, pa, pha, va, ha, kṣa
Rajasic letters:	a, ī, ṛ, ṝ, lṛ, lṝ, e, aṁ, aḥ, ka, ga, ṇa, ja, ña, ṭa, ḍa, dha, ba, bha, śa, ṣa, sa, ra, la, ḷa
Tamasic letters:	i, u, ū, ṅa, ca, cha, jha, ḍha, da, ma, ya

D. Section 3 of Varṇa Śikṣā: The Devatā, Color, and Fruit of each Letter

Having examined the alphabet, the totality of Vedic sound, in these broad strokes in sections one and two of the text, now in Section 3, the seer of the Varṇa Śikṣa examines the letters one at a time and brings out their special qualities: His first consideration is the *Devatā* for each letter.

The seer of the Varṇa Śikṣā sees these basic impulses of consciousness as impulses of organizing power, as devatās, and each devatā has a specific quality of dynamism within the wholeness: All the impulses together are like a mass of organizing power of different colors and qualities, all together creating oneness and wholeness, the way different colors come together to create white light. Seen from a distance they are like a city full of millions of people, each with his own personality and direction, but all together creating the wholeness of city life. Like that, the ocean of the impulses of consciousness, the impulses of the Veda, is seen as a city made up of so many impulses, so many devas. The Sanskrit script is called just this: *Devanāgarī*, the *Nagara,* "city," of the *Devas*, "the impulses of creative intelligence."

For the proper understanding of this, we need to understand what "devatā" actually represents. In any experience, there is a knower, that means an experiencing faculty, and there is an object of knowledge, an object of experience, and between these two, the knower and the object, there is a function, a process, which connects the two. In English, we generally describe that function which connects the knower and the known, as the "process of knowing." When we hear a sound, that structure of intelligence which hears, and by hearing brings to the experiencing faculty the knowledge of the sound, that is the "process of knowing" in that context. Whenever there is an experience, whether within the mind, or through the senses, then there is a process of knowing which mediates, bringing together the knower and the known. This process of knowing is called devatā: In Sanskrit, the knower is called Ṛṣi, the process of knowing is called Devatā, and the object of knowledge is called Chandas.

In presenting the Devatā for each letter of the alphabet, the seer is enumerating the different streams of functioning intelligence that comprise human intelligence. By human intelligence, we mean the sum total of all faculties and capabilities of knowing. All the mental functions of perception, cognition and decision-making are like the discrete channels of intelligence making up the one unbounded wholeness of infinite consciousness. The sum total of all these faculties and capabilities that comprise human intelligence is itself an experience. That is the experience when the full intelligence of the brain is harnessed and put to function. That unique style of functioning in which the total brain is put to function is called Total Brain Functioning. There is one letter, "a," which represents the unified wholeness of intelligence. Maharishi explains:

> "a" is the first Svara, the first vowel. The first vowel "a" is the flow of silence. "aaaaaaaaaaa." It is sound that carries the character of the infinite value of unified wholeness."
>
> Maharishi Mahesh Yogi, in Maharishi's Weekly Global News Conference, Jan. 15, 2003, Question 6.

The "unified wholeness" is the wholeness of all the faculties of intelligence put together. This unified wholeness is an experience in which the total brain is put to function, an experience made up of all the discrete channels of human intelligence put together. This experience of total brain functioning, Maharishi explains, is only available in the experience of transcendental consciousness, Samādhi.[8] This totality, this total brain functioning, the infinite spin of awareness in its simplest form, is the source of all the manifest point values of intelligence which make up the different values of human experience. For any thought, or any perception, any calculation, or decision, one specific part of the brain is found to be functioning, based on modern techniques of mapping blood flow in the brain using magnetic resonance imaging. Innumerable, meaning millions or perhaps even billions of point values of intelligence make up the functioning value of the human cortex. Throughout all these relative values of thought, perception and cognition, the total brain is not involved; yet there is another experience which does engage the total brain, where the entire brain is found functioning in coherence, while remaining awake and alert: This is the experience of Transcendental Consciousness. So there are isolated point values of intelligence, and there is the global value of total intelligence, total brain functioning, and these extremes are symbolized, or dynamically represented in the throat fully open sound of the vowel "a," and the throat fully closed stop of the consonant "ka."

In connecting different letters with different devatās, the seer of Varṇa Śikṣā is collecting and identifying the constituent themes or channels of intelligence which all together make up the total intelligence of every human being. The alphabet encompasses all the component channels of mind which make up the total brain functioning, and these channels of mind give rise to the different modes of excitation of the underlying field, and that field is the field of pure consciousness, the field of the Veda. This is what is meant when the seer of the Varṇa Śikṣā identifies the letter "a" as all the devatās together, "sarva-daivatyam". This letter "a" should be understood as representing or embodying total brain functioning. In the Sanskrit alphabet, the letter "a" is a part of every letter—wholeness is available at every point. That wholeness of total brain functioning is the starting point for the study of speech. Here we see that in the science of speech presented in Varṇa Śikṣā, many diverse fields are unified: Human experience of boundaries and unboundedness, and its representation in the corresponding functioning of human brain physiology, and the science of quantum field theory which sees all impulses as excitations of an underlying field, are all brought together in the one sound "a." Indeed, Vedic phonology, the Vedic science of speech, called Śikṣā, may be likened to Aristotle's "First Science," the ultimate foundation of all the sciences and arts, indeed of all disciplines founded on human intelligence: The classification of the letters of the alphabet in terms of the wholeness of human consciousness and the different channels of its expression, the different devatās, is the starting point for a universal interdisciplinary foundation for all knowledge.

Maharishi explored the fabrics of this interdisciplinary foundation for all knowledge in great depth over a period of many decades. The starting point was the correlation between pure transcendental consciousness, or Samādhi, and the vacuum state as known to quantum field theory. In a lecture in 1972 in La Antilla, Spain, called "Phonology of Creation,"[9] Maharishi explained that Parā, the transcendental level of speech in Vedic phonology, can be equated with the vacuum state in quantum field theory. In that lecture, he concluded, that if one could be awake in that field of non-activity, in the fourth state of consciousness, Transcendental Consciousness, then one would be the knower of all, the knower of everything in the field of speech, and the knower of everything in the field of existence. Then, he explained, one knows. That, he said, is the fruit of the study of Vedic phonology.

Over the course of decades of research, the flat silence of Transcendental Consciousness came to be understood as the synthesis of two values, infinite silence and infinite dynamism. The administrators of this field of silence and dynamism are the devatās: The devatās are organizing principles administering the progress and evolution of the whole universe, as well as administering the silence and dynamism of human consciousness, expressed in the flow of speech. Maharishi explained in response to questions from the press in 2005:

> These devatā: they are not concepts. They are the realities that actually perform activity in their own self-referral, eternal silence. Silence and dynamism, silence and eternal dynamism: This whole area is administered by something. And that something is the administrator. And that administrator is called devatā. And these devatā: how the devatā work? It's all inscribed in the Vedic sound—sequentially emerging sound from the state of complete silence. So this complete silence, unity, governed by the dynamism—the controller, the administrator of all diversity—is devatā. So Vedic sound, Vedic flow of intelligence, is the administrator of everything, from point to infinity. And that is within the human speech. And from that human speech, that divine intelligence and energy becomes lively and acts and reacts in the whole universe. It's a beautiful field of knowledge—the knowledge of the administration of the universe.[10]

The paradigm or world-view of Maharishi Vedic Science places human consciousness in its pure state—consciousness without any object of experience, consciousness that is awake in its own nature, pure Self-referral consciousness—at the fundamental level of administration of the entire galactic universe. The constituent elements of human speech, the phonemes or letters of the alphabet, take on the role of the fundamental organizing principles at the basis of the whole creation. In presenting the devatās for the letters, the seer of Varṇa Śikṣā presents a detailed and verifiable mapping of the constituent impulses of the ground state of human consciousness, the detailed structure of the most fundamental level of functioning of human consciousness. This mapping must be parallel to the natural laws discovered by modern physics, and this proposed correlation between physics and consciousness offers a basis for deeper understanding and further scientific investigation of the relationship of name and form in Vedic speech.

Along with the devatā of each letter, the seer of Varṇa Śikṣā also presents the color of the letter, and the special organizing power or "boon," usually called "*Phalaśruti*," that comes from the expression of that particular sound. Thus we can create a spreadsheet showing the gender, the quality of sattva, rajas or tamas, the color, the devatā, and the special organizing power or *Phalaśruti,* for every letter of the Sanskrit alphabet. (See page 87.)

The special organizing powers of some of the letters are quite amazing. Some letters give perfection, others destroy evil, some remove obstacles or destroy enemies. One gives victory, another repels death itself, and another gives the fruition of perfection. Some letters give rain, some give the fruit of one's desire. Clearly, with every word, with every letter of Sanskrit, one is bringing the descent of Heaven on Earth.

This is a tremendous knowledge. It makes each letter, each sound of Vedic speech, a golden treasure in itself. This text gives speech a new dignity, a new power, a new sense of greatness. Every letter of the Sanskrit alphabet is an expression of the Divine Being, it is the gift of God to man. Every letter is a particle of Heaven made manifest on earth. This knowledge is the gift of this seer of the Vedāṅga Śikṣā, the unnamed seer of Varṇa Ṣikṣā. Truly, this text is one of the greatest blessings in the field of Śikṣā.

E. The Seer of Varṇa Śikṣā

Maharishi has said that we give special tribute to the seers of the Vedāṅgas, because they were able to see the fine details of the process of formation of the flow of sound of the Vedas, and that required much greater purity of awareness than the cognition of the ṛcas of the Vedas themselves. All glory to the great purity and clarity of cognition of the seer of Varṇa Śikṣā!

> Some Vedic seers just cognized the hymns and did not bother to bring out any details of their structuring. The seers of the Vedāṅgas, however, cognized the detailed mechanics which lie between the expressed value of sound and pure consciousness, the mechanics of what is happening to consciousness at that moment, of what aspect of creative intelligence is functioning at what level, and of the sequential emergence of sound after sound. Greater credit should be given to this latter group of seers who cognized the mechanics of how the hymns were structured. Very great credit is due to that sharp enlightened vision which could locate specific knowledge about the structuring of manifest creation on the level of consciousness and bring out in understandable language these signposts on the path for seekers of knowledge.

(Student summmary of) Maharishi's Vedic Studies Core Course: "Lesson 6: The Eternity of the Veda: Preservation Embedded in the Nature of Life," 1974.

This text, which we call "Varṇa Śikṣā," is written in Telugu script on palm leaves: http://tinyurl.com/pkdan9t

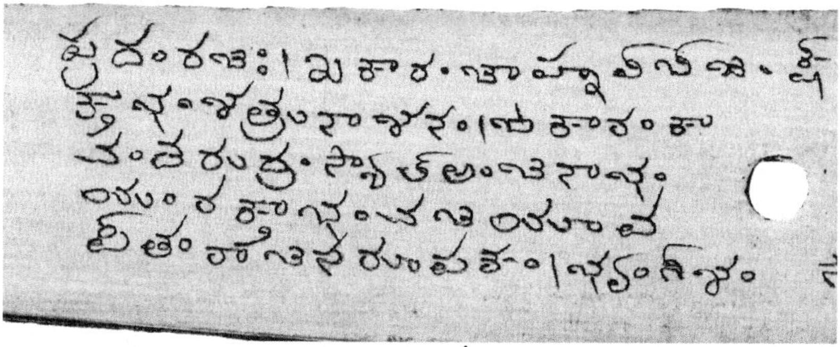

Close-up of Varṇa Śikṣā palm leaf

It is an enigma, a mystery to say the least. The name of the seer is not mentioned, and there is no colophon or summary statement at the end naming the text, so we do not know it's name. We believe it to be a Śikṣā text because it is found in the middle of a bundle of other Śikṣā texts. It was catalogued as "Varṇa-liṅgādi-nirṇaya," which means that the cataloguer noticed that it deals with *Varṇa*, letters, and starts with a discussion of the gender (*Liṅga*) of letters. This is apt, but somewhat superficial. What is the text as a whole about, what is its purpose? The cataloguer indicates that the text is incomplete. But beyond the absence of a colophon, it's incompleteness is itself a conjecture: The third and last section goes through the alphabet, letter by letter, and reaching the end of the alphabet, and thereby bringing complete fulfillment to that investigation, the text ends. Moreover, there are exactly 48 verses in the text as a whole, the same number as the letters of the alphabet from "a" to "ha," (not counting "ḹ") so there is a sense of completion on that level also. If we put a full stop at that ending point, we find ourselves in possession of a systematic and comprehensive analysis of the letters of the alphabet, presenting the gender, the quality of sattva, rajas or tamas, the color, and the devatā of each letter, as well as the benefit or boon of many of the letters. The spreadsheet of qualities and characteristics of the letters seems quite complete, so we are inclined to take issue with the cataloguer on this point regarding the completeness of the text.

As to the absence of knowledge of the seer of this text, this may point to a characteristic that applies to the whole field of Śikṣā: There is a large body of cognitions of Śikṣā that have been passed down for generations, the origins, that is the names of the seers of the verses having been long forgotten. We call this "lore," and this body of lore may also account for the phenomenon of shared verses between so many Śikṣā texts. If a Śikṣā writer was familiar with the lore of Śikṣā, he would naturally make use of various verses that were appropriate for the unfoldment of his theme, with the knowledge that they carried with them a great authenticity, having been time-tested and handed down for countless generations. Other Śikṣā writers might also use the same verses, oblivious of the fact that another writer had included those verses in his text, because they were part of the lore of Śikṣā, and belonged to everyone. As more and more Śikṣā were written down as texts, verses originating from the general lore of Śikṣā could show up multiple times, occurring even in Śikṣā belonging to different Vedas. We take the phenomenon of shared verses as evidence for the existence of a great lore of Śikṣā verses, and we take this unnamed and unsigned work of Śikṣā to be a part of that lore of Śikṣā.

F. The Unique Contribution of Varṇa Śikṣā

In Maharishi's expression, it is the glory of speech that it is capable of binding the boundless.

> Speech is able to sing the glory of the infinite unbounded. The Ṛg Veda sings the glory of speech in supreme terms, saying that it is the power of speech that is able to bind the boundless.[11]

Speech is capable of giving tangible expression to that which is beyond boundaries, ineffable. All the glorious expressions of the experience of the Divine in the religious texts of all the great religions of the world make use of language, speech, to give expression to the infinite Divine consciousness, to make evident the essence of Godhead, the ultimate source of energy and intelligence in all creation. How is it possible that speech can give expression to the infinite inexpressible ultimate source of all creation?

In the classical atomistic view of creation, creation is made of layers. Particles, such as electrons, neutrons and protons combine together to form atoms. Different kinds of atoms, carbon, hydrogen, nitrogen and oxygen, etc. come together to form molecules, and then molecules come together to form cells, and cells join together to form multi-celled organisms, and more and more complex organelles and organs are built up, and then eventually a human being is created. Somehow, from all of these lifeless elements, electrons, protons, atoms and so forth, life is created, intelligence is created, as if at the very end of the process of creation, life is bestowed on lifeless matter.

The author of Varṇa Śikṣā is showing us a different scenario for the creation of speech, speech that is capable of binding the boundless. The simplest sound, the sound "a," is the infinite frequency wave function of total knowledge and total organizing power, and all the other letters are an aspect, a part, an image, or shadow of that holistic knowledge and organizing power. Each Sanskrit letter has "a" at its source, each letter contains "a" within it, so each letter has the infinite pure consciousness through and through: Each letter is full of Divine Life. So when for example in the Upanishads, the Glory and Majesty of the supreme Brahman is extolled, and the greatness of the Divine is unfolded, the verbal expression of that greatness is not made up of dead points of lifeless inert vibration, but rather, each letter is full of Divine Life, full of infinite consciousness, woven warp and woof with the sparks of unbounded intelligence at the basis of the whole creation. This is the purport of Varṇa Śikṣā, this is the universal and timeless message that it seeks to convey to the student: Vedic speech in its very essence, letter by letter is always the expression of the infinite, the signpost of the Divine, the hallmark of totality. Every letter is telling the story of wholeness of life, every letter points to the infinite wellsprings of energy and intelligence at the basis of creation, every letter is in its essential nature a messenger, a representative of the Divine.

G. The Relationship of Name and Form in Varṇa Śikṣā

Varṇa Śikṣā may be the only Śikṣā which exposes the dynamics of the relationship between name and form. By highlighting the different qualities of the letter, the gender, the qualities of sattva, rajas and tamas, the different colors, and the different principles of organizing power, this Śikṣā presents a mapping of the fine mechanics of the process of creation. The one unbounded ocean of consciousness locates silence and dynamism within its own nature, and then on the ground of this duality, three basic tendencies, sattva, rajas and tamas emerge; these three are further expressed as four colors, and then from there the qualities of the 50 letters of the Sanskrit alphabet, and finally, on that basis, the infinite diversity of forms and phenomena in creation. The seed of multiplicity is contained in the many letters of the alphabet with their different qualities, and the different qualities of the letters emerge from the relationship between "a" and "ka"—"a" which is sarva-daivatya, all the devatās, all the unlimited power of total natural law, and "ka," which is the point value of the infinite organizing power of all the devatās, that point value expressed as "giving rain," and thereby making manifest and concretely visible the abstract organizing power of total natural law and thus creating the multiplicity of all the diverse beings in creation.

There is a changing value in creation, an ever-evolving, ever-transforming, ever creating flow of natural law expressing itself in sequential steps of silence and dynamism. This ever-flowing stream of Natural Law ever-moving in the evolutionary direction, is captured in language: Language is versatile, it moves, it flows, and in flowing, it is capable of grasping the ever-flowing dynamism of the cosmic force of evolution. But in that flow, there is also a non-moving junction point. This non-move is not captured in speech. Rather, the non-move is expressed in terms of number systems and equations. Language and number systems thus deal with two different worlds or realms of experience, the ever-flowing, ever-changing, and the non-flowing, absolutely non-flexible junction point or balancing point of flow. But even the absolute non-flexibility of number systems can be captured in speech by connecting words with specific numbers. This concept was demonstrated in the Iṅgya Ratnam, a Śikṣā text which counts the number of separable compounds in each Anuvāka of the Taittirīya Saṁhitā using the Kaṭapay system of assigning letters to numbers. In Varṇa Śikṣā, seven verses demonstrate a system of representing numbers in speech in which full words are assigned each numeral. The word assignments are as follows:

1	Śiva	2	Pakṣa
3	Agni	4	Veda, Abdhi
5	Bhūta, Bāṇa, Artha	6	Rasa
7	Gṛha	8	Vasu
10	Dik	11	Rudra
12	Bhānu	14	Manu
15	Tithi	16	Kalā, Śaivādhikārakāḥ

Following this system of representing numbers, common in ancient Indian paleography,[12] the numbers 1 to 16 are presented in Varṇa Śikṣā using the words traditionally associated with those numbers, and then these words are associated numerically with the 16 vowels in Sanskrit language.

1	a	2	ā	3	i	4	ī
5	u	6	ū	7	ṛ	8	ṝ
9	lṛ	10	lṝ	11	e	12	ai
13	o	14	au	15	aṁ	16	aḥ

In this way, these words become a kind of "shorthand" for referring to specific vowels. In making use of this system to divide and classify the vowels, the author of Varṇa Śikṣā is demonstrating the use of speech to represent non-changing, eternal abstract entities. This exposes a completely different aspect of the relationship of name and form.

The purpose of presenting vowels in two different ways, first with words representing numbers in sections 1 and 2; and then secondly, with the traditional notation, giving the letter followed by the word "kāra," signifying the doer or maker of that sound, *i.e.* the letter, seems to be for the pegagogical purpose of unfolding the deep structure of the relationship of name and form. This may also account for the somewhat tedious presentations of qualities of letters, each mapping being expressed two times, each time in a somewhat different way. There may have been a more economical way to present the specifics of the knowledge of the characteristics of the letters of the alphabet, but the author's intent was deeper: He wanted the student to have also a practical example of different features of the relationship of name and form, brought out by bringing to light both moving and unmoving aspects of Natural Law.

The use of words to represent numbers that represent vowels, thereby exposing the inner dynamics of the relationship of name and form, is a brilliant tour de force of the writer, unfolding a deeper reality of the fine mechanics of creation in broad and clear strokes. There is a lesson that there are multiple layers of meaning in every Vedic text, and these are all intentional, simultaneously valid perspectives of the reality of the text.

The abstract relationship of name and form, sound and meaning, is made tangible for the first time in this mapping of the qualities of the different letters. Here we see the detailed fabrics of the eternal relationship between name and form. This is the essence, the soul of Śikṣā. Varṇa Śikṣā, unnamed and unsigned, hits the target of what Śikṣā really is and what a Śikṣā text should be: At the threshold between unity and diversity, it provides the lamp at the door which connects all the innumerable forms and phenomena in creation with their source in the sounds of the Veda. Illuminating the infinite frequency of the most simple sine wave, represented by the sound "a" as it is being transformed into two values, (gender,) then three values (sattva, rajas and tamas), then four values (represented by colors, principally red, white, black and yellow) and then all the different qualities represented by all the different letters, Varṇa Śikṣā shows how wholeness can flow in waves of multiplicity while remaining connected to the source of all diversity, the oneness of universal Being. Varṇa Śikṣā teaches the Divine glory of the alphabet, it unfolds the dignity of human speech, it connects the abstract essence of the Divine with manifest creation, and invites the student on a journey of discovery, locating total knowledge and total organizing power within himself. This is ideal education, and this is the essence of Śikṣā, taught by an unnamed seer. This is truly a priceless jewel of wisdom, a rare gem in the treasury of human knowledge.

Notes

1. Maharishi's commentaries on the fundamental principles of Śikṣā, Vedic phonology, with reference to the Sanskrit alphabet, are summarized in Freund, Peter F., *Vedic literature reading curriculum.* Ann Arbor, Mich.: Dissertation Information Service, 2006. "Chapter 2: The Vedic Alphabet," available here: http://www.peterffreund.com/Dissertation/Freund_Dissertation_02_Vedic_Alphabet.pdf.

2. See: http://is1.mum.edu/vedicreserve/shiksha/atreya_shiksha.pdf, p.2.

3. Sandal, Mohan Lal, *The Mīmāmsā Sūtras of Jaimini*, AMS Press: New York, 1979, p2. (Untranslated Sanskrit words translated for clarity.)

4. See: http://is1.mum.edu/vedicreserve/darshanas/Yoga/yoga_darshanam.pdf

5. See *Invincible America Assembly Experiences of Higher States of Consciousness*, MUM Press: Fairfield, Iowa, 2012.

6. "The Unmanifest Home of Creative Intelligence," May 2, 1976, Seelisberg, Switzerland, videotaped lecture in *Core Course on Invincibility, Theme 10*, MERU, 1978.

7. "The Structure of Pure Knowledge," Part 3, July 29, 1979, Seelisberg, Switzerland, YouTube: http://www.youtube.com/watch?v=VJqM_2Q6LwI.

8. "The Origin of True Genius," Maharishi's Global News Conference, May 14, 2003, Vlodrop, Holland, YouTube: http://www.youtube.com/watch?v=Qu3oqlYO268.

9. "Phonology of Creation," La Antilla, Spain, 26 December 1972, IAASCI.

10. "The Importance of the Sun in Sthapatya Veda," August 10, 2005, Vlodrop, Holland, Maharishi's Global News Conferences.

11. "Science of Creative Intelligence and Speech," Lesson 25 of *Science of Creative Intelligence Teacher Training Course*, Spring, 1972, Fuiggi, Italy, MIU Press, p.4.

12. Burnell, A.C., *Elements of South-Indian Paleography from the fourth to the seventeenth century A.D., being an introduction to the study of South-Indian inscriptions and manuscripts*, New Delhi: Asian Educational Services, 1994.

40 Branches of Vedic Literature

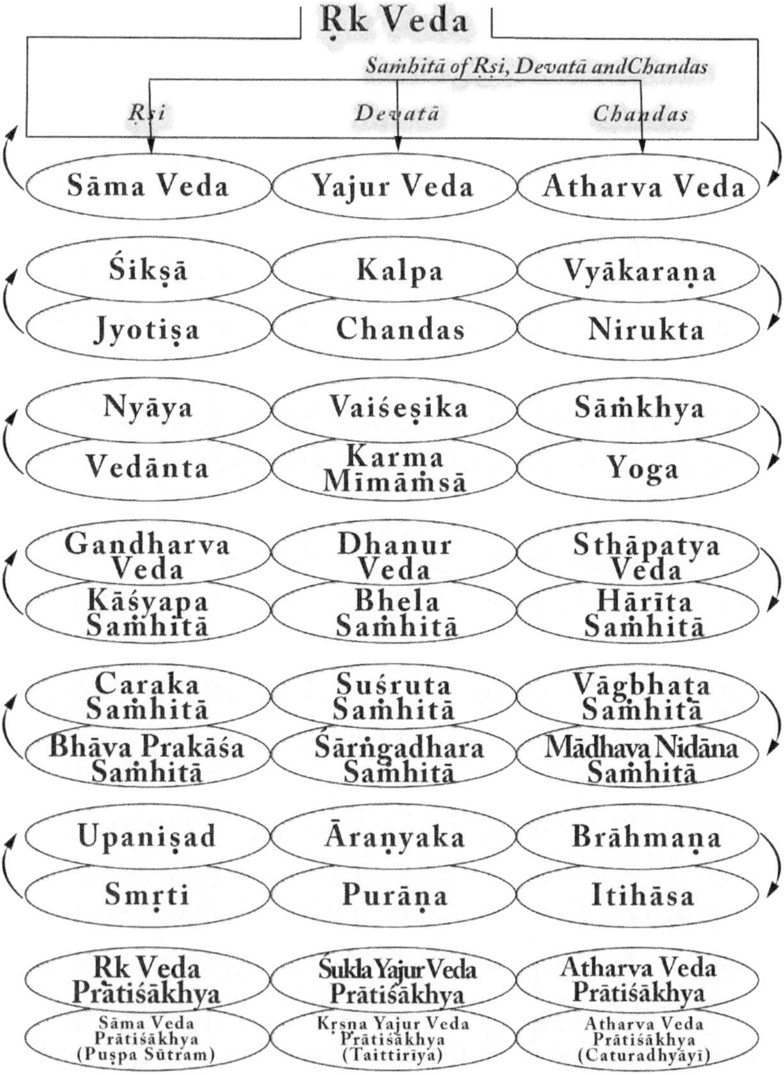
Ṛk Veda
Saṁhitā of Ṛṣi, Devatā andChandas
Ṛṣi
Devatā
Chandas
Sāma Veda
Yajur Veda
Atharva Veda
Śikṣā
Kalpa
Vyākaraṇa
Jyotiṣa
Chandas
Nirukta
Nyāya
Vaiśeṣika
Sāṁkhya
Vedānta
Karma Mīmāṁsā
Yoga
Gandharva Veda
Dhanur Veda
Sthāpatya Veda
Kāśyapa Saṁhitā
Bhela Saṁhitā
Hārīta Saṁhitā
Caraka Saṁhitā
Suśruta Saṁhitā
Vāgbhaṭa Saṁhitā
Bhāva Prakāśa Saṁhitā
Śārṅgadhara Saṁhitā
Mādhava Nidāna Saṁhitā
Upaniṣad
Āraṇyaka
Brāhmaṇa
Smṛti
Purāṇa
Itihāsa
Rk Veda Prātiśākhya
Śukla Yajur Veda Prātiśākhya
Atharva Veda Prātiśākhya
Sāma Veda Prātiśākhya (Puṣpa Sūtram)
Kṛṣṇa Yajur Veda Prātiśākhya (Taittirīya)
Atharva Veda Prātiśākhya (Caturadhyāyī)

Varṇa Śikṣā Translation

वर्णशिक्षा

वर्णानां स्त्रीपुंनपुंसकसंज्ञा

Section 1: Gender of Letters

ककारं च गकारं च चकारं च जकारकम्
टकारं च डकारं च तकारं च दकारकम् १
पकारं च बकारं च षकारं च क्षकारकम्
एते द्वादशवर्णाः स्युः पुंल्लिङ्गाश्चेति कीर्तिताः २

1-2. ka, ga, ca, ja, ṭa, ḍa, ta, da, pa, ba, ṣa, kṣa, these twelve letters are known as masculine.

खकारं च घकारं च छकारं च झकारकम्
ठकारं च ढकारं च थकारं च धकारकम् ३
फकारं च भकारं च शकारं च सकारकम्
एते वै भानुबीजानि जायाश्चेति प्रकीर्तिताः ४

3-4. kha, gha, cha, jha, ṭha, ḍha, tha, dha, pha, bha, śa, sa, these twelve letters are known as feminine.

शेषं नपुंसकं ज्ञेयं त्रयो भेदा इति स्मृताः ५

5. The rest are known as neuter. These three divisions, (masculine, feminine and neuter,) have been handed down by tradition.

शिवाग्निभूतरुद्राश्च त्रयोदश तिथिस्तथा
एते वै स्वरवर्णाः स्युः पुंल्लिङ्गाश्चेति कीर्तिताः

6. Śiva (1="a"), Agni (3="i"), Bhūta (5="u") and Rudra (11="e"), the thirteenth (13="o"), and the Tithi (15="aṁ") similarly.
Indeed, these vowels, a, i, u, e, o, and aṁ, should be known as masculine.

पक्षो वेदरसा भानुर्मनुशैवाधिकारकाः
एतानि स्वरवर्णानि स्त्रीलिङ्गानीति कीर्त्यते

7. Pakṣa (2="ā"), Veda (4="ī"), Rasa (6="ū"), Bhānu (12="ai"), Manu (14="au"), Śaivādhikārakāḥ (16="aḥ")
These vowels, ā, ī, ū, ai, au, and aḥ, are known as feminine.

प्रकृतिः सप्तवर्णानि विकृतिस्तु नवार्णकम्
प्रकृतिर्ह्रस्वमित्युक्तं विकृतिर्दीर्घमुच्यते ८

8. Seven vowels are said to be Prakṛti (a, i, u, ṛ, lṛ, aṁ, aḥ); nine vowels are said to be vikṛti (ā, ī, ū, ṝ, lṝ, e, ai, o, au).
The Prakṛti vowels are said to be short; the vikṛti vowels are said to be long.

प्रथमाश्च तृतीयाश्च षकारश्च क्षकारकम्
एते द्वादशवर्णाः स्युः पुंल्लिङ्गाश्चेति कीर्तिताः

9. (In review:) The first letter of each varga, (ka, ca, ṭa, ta, pa), and the third letter of each varga, (ga, ja, ḍa, da, ba, and) ṣa and kṣa,
These twelve letters are known to be masculine.

द्वितीयाश्च चतुर्थाश्च शसकारौ तथैव च
एते द्वादशवर्णाः स्युः स्त्रील्लिङ्गाश्चेति
प्रकीर्तिताः

10. The second letter of each varga, (kha, cha, ṭha, tha, pha) and the fourth letter of each varga, (gha, jha, ḍha, dha, bha) and also śa, and sa,
These twelve letters are known to be feminine.

अन्तस्थाश्चोत्तमाश्चैव ऋ ऌ वर्णौ तथैव च
हकारश्च ळकारश्च क्लीबाश्चेति प्रकीर्तिताः ११

11. Semi-vowels (ya, ra, la, and va) and the last letters of each varga, (i.e. the nasals, ṅa, ña, ṇa, na, ma), as also the two letters ṛ (and ṝ) and lṛ (and lṝ), and the letters ha and ḷa are known to be neuter.

वर्णानां सत्वरजस्तमो गुणाः

Section 2: Qualities of Sattva, Rajas and Tamas of the Letters

पक्षो गृहार्थसंख्या च त्रयोदशमनुस्तथा
एते वै सात्त्विकगुणाः श्वेतवर्णा तथैव च १२

12. Pakṣa (2="ā"), Gṛha (7) + Artha (5) counted together (12="ai"), the thirteenth (13="o"), and Manu (14="au") similarly,
These letters, ā, ai, o, and au have the quality of sattva, and are white in color.

शिवाब्धिसप्ता वसुदिक्च रुद्राः तिथिश्चैव कलास्तथा
एते वै राजसगुणा रक्तवर्णा तथैव च १३

13. Śiva (1="a"), Abdhi (4="ī"), seven (7="ṛ"), Vasu (8="ṝ"), Dik (10="ḷrī"), Rudra (11="e"), Tithi (15="aṁ"), Kalā (16="aḥ")
The letters a, ī, ṛ, ṝ, ḷrī, e, aṁ, and aḥ have the quality of rajas, and are red in color.

बाणो रसस्तृतीया च श्यामवर्णा तमोगुणाः

14-1. Bāṇa (5="u"), Rasa (6="ū"), and the third (3="i"), [the letters i, u, and ū] have the quality of tamas, and are black in color.

हल्

द्वितीया च चतुर्थश्च तवर्गप्रथमोत्तमौ १४

14-2. Now with regard to consonants: The second letters of vargas (kha, ṭha, tha, pha) and the fourth letter of [the first] varga (gha); the first and last letters of ta-varga (ta, na);

पवर्गप्रथमश्चैव वेदाष्टादश एव च

एते वै सात्विकगुणाः श्वेतवर्णं तथैव च १५

15. And the first letter of the pa-varga (pa), [and among the letters following the pa varga] the fourth letter (Veda=4)(va), the eighth letter (ha) and the tenth letter (kṣa).

These have the quality of sattva and are white in color.

खकारं च घकारं च ठकारं च थकारकम्

तकारं च नकारं च पकारं च फकारकम्

वकारं च हकारश्च क्षकारं चेति सात्विकः १६

16. (In review:) The letters kha, gha, ṭha, tha, ta, na, pa, pha, va, ha, and kṣa, are sattvic.

कवर्गप्रथमश्चैव टवर्गश्च तथैव च

तृतीयाश्च तपवर्गचतुर्थाश्च चटवर्गोत्तमौ तथा

17. The first letter of the ka-varga and the ṭa-varga

(ka, ṭa); the third letter of vargas (ga, ja, ḍa, ba); the fourth letter of the ta-varga and the pa-varga (dha, bha); the last letter of the ca-varga and the ṭa-varga (ña and ṇa);

ऊष्माणश्चैव रेफश्च लळकारौ रजोगुणाः
कवर्गप्रथमश्चैव टवर्गश्च तथैव च १८

18. The sibilants (śa, ṣa, sa), repha (ra), and the letters la and ḷa have the qualities of rajas.
(To review:) The first letter of the ka-varga and the ṭa-varga (ka, ṭa);

तृतीयाश्च भकारश्च धकारं च ञकारकम्
णकारं चोष्मणश्चैव रेफश्चैव लळौ तथा
एते रजोगुणाः प्रोक्ता रक्तवर्णां तथैव च १९

19. The third letter of vargas (ga, ja, ḍa, ba); the letters bha, dha, and ña;
The letter ṇa, the sibilants, repha (ra), and the letters la and ḷa are said to have the quality of rajas and to be red in color.

चकारश्च द्वितीया च ङकारं च मकारकम् २०

20. The letter ca, and the second letter of the ca varga (cha), the letters ṅa, and ma.

ढकारं च दकारं च यकारं च झकारकम्

तामसः कृष्णवर्णा च उत्तमश्च मिश्रकम् २१

21. The letters ḍha, da, ya, and jha have the quality of tamas and are dark blue/black in color.

चकारश्च द्वितीया च आद्यन्तौ वर्गपञ्चमौ
चटवर्गचतुर्थौ च तवर्गश्च तृतीयकम् २२

22. (To review the tamasic letters:) The letter ca, and the second letter of the ca varga (cha), the fifth letter of the first and last vargas (ṅa, ma),
The fourth letters of the ca-varga and ṭa-varga (jha, ḍha), and the third letter of the ta-varga (da);

यकारस्तामसगुणाः श्यामवर्णास्तथैव च २३

23. And the letter ya are tamasic in quality and black in color.

Section 3: Devatās, Colors, and Qualities of Each Letter

अकारं सर्वदैवत्यं रक्तवर्णं रजः स्मृतम्
आकारः स्यात्पराशक्तिः श्वेतं सात्विकमुच्यते

24. The letter "a" is all the devatās, red in color, and traditionally known to be rajasic in quality.
The letter "ā" should be known as Parāśakti, and is said to be white in color and sattvic in quality.

इकारं विष्णुदैवत्यं श्यामं तामसमुच्यते
मायाशक्तिरितीकारं पीतं राजसमुच्यते २५

25. The letter "i" is Viṣṇu devatā, and is said to be black in color, and tamasic in quality.
Māyā-śakti is the letter "ī", it is said to be yellow in color, and rajasic in quality.

उकारं वास्तुदैवत्यं कृष्णं तामसमीरितम्
ऊकारं भूमिदैवत्यं श्यामळं तामसं भवेत् २६

26. The letter "u" is the Vāstu devatā, and is proclaimed to be black in color, and tamasic in quality.
The letter "ū" is the Earth (bhūmi) devatā, black in color and tamasic in quality.

ऋकारं ब्रह्मणो ज्ञेयं पीतं राजसमुच्यते
शिखण्डिरूपं ॠकारं राजसं पीतवर्णकम् २७

27. The letter "ṛ" is known as Brahman, it is said to be yellow in color and rajasic in quality.
The letter "ṝ" has the form of Śikhaṇḍin, is yellow in color and rajasic in quality.

अश्विनौ तु ऌ ॡ प्रोक्तौ
एकारं वीरभद्रं स्याद्रजः पीतं तु सिद्धिदम्

28. The letters "lṛ" and "lṝ" are said to be the two

Aśvins.
The letter "e" should be understood as Vīrabhadra, it is rajasic in quality, yellow in color, and bestows siddhis (siddhidam).

ऐकारं वाग्भवं विन्द्यात्

ओकारमीश्वरं विन्द्याज्ज्योतिः सत्वं फलप्रदम्

29. The letter "ai" should be known as the vital essence of speech (vāgbhava).
The letter "o" should be understood as Īśvara, pure light (*Jyoti*) in color, sattvic in quality, bestowing fruit.

औकारमादिशक्तिः स्याच्छुक्लं सर्वत्र सिद्धिदम्

अंकारं तु महेशं स्याद्रक्तवर्णं तु राजसम् ३०

30. The letter "au" is the primordial creative power, Ādi-śakti, it is white in color, and gives perfection in every area (sarvatra siddhida).
The letter "aṁ" should be understood as Maheśa, red in color, and rajasic in quality.

अः कारं कालरुद्रं च रक्तं राजसमुच्यते

प्राजापत्यं ककारं स्यात्पीतं वृष्टिप्रदं रजः ३१

31. The letter "aḥ" is Kāla-rudra, and is said to be red in color and rajasic in quality.

Prajāpati should be taken as the devatā of the letter "ka," it is yellow in color, rain-bestowing, and rajasic.

खकारं जाह्नवीबीजं क्षीराभं पापनाशनम्
गाणपत्यं गकारं स्याद्रक्ताभं विघ्ननाशनम् ३२

32. The letter "kha" is the seed from which Mother Gaṅgā, (Jāhnavī) springs, it is milk-white in color, and destroys evils.
Gaṇapati (known as Gaṇeśa) should be understood to be the devatā of the letter "ga," it is red in color and destroys obstacles (vighna-nāśanam).

घकारं भैरवं ज्ञेयं मुक्ताभं शत्रुनाशनम्
ङकारं कालबीजं स्यात्कालं तार्क्ष्यं समुच्यते

33. The letter "gha" should be known to be Bhairava, pearl-white in color, and enemy-destroying.
The letter "ṅa" should be understood as Time, black (kāla) in color, and said to be Tārkṣya.

चकारं चण्डरुद्रं स्यात् अञ्जनाभं तु तामसम्
छकारं भद्रकाळी स्यात्तामसं परिकीर्तितम् ३४

34. The letter "ca" should be understood as Caṇḍarudra, collyrium-colored (black), and tamasic in quality.
The letter "cha" should be understood as Bhadrakāḷī, tamasic in quality, and proclaiming all around.

जकारं जम्भहा ज्ञेयं रक्ताभं च जयावहम्

झकारमर्धनारीशं श्यामरक्तं तु मिश्रकम् ३५

35. The letter "ja" is to be known as Jambhahā, red in color and bringing victory (jayāvaham).
The letter "jha" is hermaphrodite Śiva, (half male, half female,) and mixed black and red in color.

ञकारं सर्पदैवत्यं पीतं राजसरूपकम्

भृङ्गीशं स्याट्टकारं तु रक्तं राजसमेव च ३६

36. The letter "ña" is the Snake Devatā (sarpadaivatya), yellow in color, and rajasic in appearance (rājasarūpaka).
The letter "ṭa" should be understood as Bhṛṅgīśa, red in color and rajasic in quality.

ठकारं चन्द्रबीजं स्याच्छ्वेतं सात्त्विकमुच्यते

डकारं चैकनेत्रं स्यात्पीतं राजसमुच्यते ३७

37. The letter "ṭha" is the Moon, said to be white in color and sattvic in quality.
The letter "ḍa" should be understood as (the *Vidyeśvara*) Ekanetra, "one-eyed," and is said to be yellow in color, and rajasic in quality.

ढकारं यमबीजं स्यान्नीलं मृत्युविनाशनम्

णकारं नन्दिबीजं स्याद्रक्ताभं चार्थसिद्धिदम्

38. The letter "ḍha" should be understood to have Yama as its devatā, blue-black (nīla) in color, and destroying death.
The letter "ṇa" should be understood as Nandi, red in color, bestowing fulfillment of every goal (artha-siddhida).

तकारं वास्तुदैवत्यं श्वेतं

थकारं ब्रह्मणो ज्ञेयं

दुर्गाबीजं दकारं स्याच्छ्यामं सर्वार्थसिद्धिदम्

39. The letter "ta" is the Vāstu-devatā, white in color.
The letter "tha" should be known as Brahman.
The letter "da" should be understood as Durgā, black in color, granting mastery of all things (sarva-artha-siddhi-da).

धकारं धनदं प्रोक्तं पीताभं चार्थसिद्धिदम्

नकारं चैव सावित्री स्फाटिकं पापनाशनम्

40. The letter "dha" is said to bestow wealth, it is yellow in color, and bestows accomplishment of the goal.
The letter "na" should be understood as Sāvitrī, crystalline in color, and destroying evil.

पकारं चैव पर्जन्यं शुक्लाभं वृष्टिसिद्धिदम्

फकारं पाशुपत्यं च सत्वः पापविनाशनम्

41. The letter "pa" should be understood as the devatā of rain, (Parjanya,) white in color, and granting perfection in rain.
The letter "pha" is the lord of cattle (Paśupati), sattvic in quality, destroying evil.

बकारं तु त्रिमूर्तिः स्यात्पीतं सर्वार्थसिद्धिदम्
भकारं भार्गवं विन्द्याद्रक्तं भाग्यप्रदं भवेत् ४२

42. The letter "ba" should be understood as (the *Vidyeśvara*) Trimūrti, yellow in color, granting mastery of all things.
The letter "bha" should be understood as Bhārgava, red in color, and bestowing good fortune.

मकारं मदनं विन्द्याच्छ्यामं कामफलप्रदम्
यकारं वायुदैवत्यं कृष्णामुच्चाटनं भवेत् ४३

43. The letter "ma" is known as the god of love, black in color, and bestowing the fruit of one's desire.
The letter "ya" is the devatā Vāyu, black in color, and destroying enemies.

रकारं वह्निदैवत्यं रक्ताभं राजसं भवेत्
लकारं पृथिवीबीजं पीतं स्यात् लम्भनं भवेत्

44. The letter "ra" is the devatā of all conveyances (vahni-daivatya), red in color, rajasic in quality.

The letter "la" should be understood as the earth element (Pṛthivī), yellow in color, characterized by attainment.

वकारं वारुणं बीजं शुक्लाभं योगनाशनम्
लक्ष्मीबीजं शकारं स्यात् हेमाभं राजसं भवेत्

45. The letter "va" is the devatā Varuṇa, white in color, annihilating relative boundaries through union with the unbounded field of pure intelligence.
The letter "śa" is the devatā Lakṣmī, the color of gold, and rajasic in quality.

षकारं द्वादशात्मं स्यात् रक्ताभं तु जयप्रदम्
सकारं शक्तिबीजं स्याद्रक्तं स्थितिकरं भवेत्

46. The letter "ṣa" should be understood as the soul of the twelve (Jyotirliṅgas), red in color, and bestowing victory.
The letter "sa" should be understood as śakti, (power,) red in color, creating stability.

हकारं शिवबीजं स्याच्छुद्धस्फटिकसन्निभम्
अणिमाद्यष्टसिद्धं च भुक्तिं मुक्तिं प्रयच्छति

47. The letter "ha" should be understood as Śiva, pure crystalline white in color, granting the eight principle spiritual powers (siddhis)—*aṇimā*, minute body;

mahimā, huge body; *garimā*, heavy body; *laghimā,* lightness of body including yogic flying; *prāpti*, ability to attain any desired object; *prākāmya*, irresistible will; *Īśitva*, mastery of creation; and *vaśitva*, subduing everything to onc's will—and bestowing all enjoyments of the relative field, as well as eternal liberation.

47-2. From the collapse of the first letter, "a," to its own infinitesimal point, there are eight complete turns or somersaults: Through those somersaults one experiences everything that there is to be experienced (bhukti) and realizes everything that there is to be known (mukti).

ळकारं चात्मबीजं स्याद्रक्ताभं सर्वसिद्धिदम्

४८

48. The letter "ḷa" should be understood as Ātmā, red in color, bestowing all powers.

[इति वर्णशिक्षा समाप्ता]

End of Varṇa Śikṣā

Colors of the Letters of the Sanskrit Alphabet According to Varṇa Śikṣā

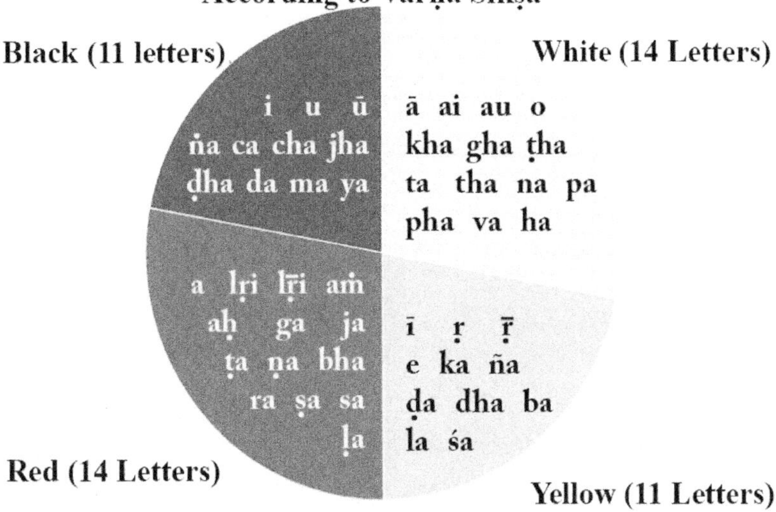

The Devatās of Varṇa Śikṣā

अ A is *Sarvadaivatya*, all the devatās. The total intelligence of Natural Law is represented by “a”, which is the first syllable of Ṛgveda, the seed out of which the entire Ṛgveda and the whole of Vedic literature is systematically and sequentially unfolded: “a” contains within itself the total knowledge and organizing power—the sum total of all the devatās.

आ Ā is Parāśakti, the supreme Śakti or power. All the different powers, including Jñānaśakti, power of knowledge, and Kriyāśakti, power of action, are derived from Parāśakti, the supreme Śakti, or energy of the Transcendental Being at the basis of the whole creation.

इ I is Viṣṇu, the supreme God, the maintainer and administrator of creation. He is often depicted as reclining on a serpent at the bottom of the ocean. In his four hands are a lotus, a discus, a mace and a conch. There are 10 incarnations of Viṣṇu, as a fish, a tortoise, a boar, a man-lion, a dwarf, Paraśurāma, Rāma, Kṛṣṇa, Buddha and Kalki.

> Viṣṇu is provided with a tiara, armlets and bracelets; he is adorned with a hip girdle and other ornaments and his clothing is yellow. He has four arms and (his anterior hands make) the gesture of bestowing and that of absence of fear whilst, (in the other two), he holds the conch and the discus. He is immaculate. Whether he is standing or

seated, Avanī is on his left, and Ramā is on his right. He is on a throne or is on a lotus; dark in color he is immovable and shining. It is said that the radiance of Śrilakṣmī and Bhūmi makes him shine and that his eyes are like lotuses. This is the one image that is to be installed by the sages for those who seek liberation. Garuḍa is said to be his emblem and his mount. Mayamatam 36: 8-12[1].

ई Ī is Māyā Śakti, the power which creates this whole illusory, ever-changing creation. Whereas the one unchanging infinite eternal Being alone is real, by the power of Māyā, the infinite unchanging eternal unmanifest Being is seen as the ever-changing manifest universe. The creative power of Mother Divine, Māyā Śakti, creates this grand illusion which hides the unmanifest eternal reality of Being.

उ U is Vāstu Daivatya. Vāstu is the principle of architectural design which connects the individual expression of Natural Law with the intelligence of the cosmos. When the organization of space and form in the layout of houses, towns, cities, gardens, roads, water works, shops and public areas is completely in accordance with Total Natural Law, so that moving about in those structures the individual enjoys complete support of Natural Law, then that structure, form or space exhibits the quality of Vāstu. Vāstu is that intelligence of Nature which spontaneously computes perfection in the field of action through alignment with Total Natural Law on the material level.

ऊ Ū is Bhūmi Daivatya. Bhūmi is Mother Earth, an aspect of Mother Divine. "She is depicted in votive statuary, seated on a square platform which rests on the back of four elephants representing the four directions of the world. When depicted with four arms, she holds a pomegranate, a water vessel, a bowl containing healing herbs, and another containing vegetables."[2]

> Bhūmi is dark like an ear of wheat and her eyes are big like lotuses; she has big eyes, wears the mark on her forehead and her hair is curly. She is adorned with all jewels and has a flower in her hand and she is beautiful, her tiara shines. She who supports all beings, is dressed in yellow and is seated on a throne. (Mayamatam 36:274-275)[3]

ऋ Ṛ is Brahman. Brahman is the supreme realization, the goal of Vedānta, the highest attainment. It is Total Knowledge and Total Organizing Power, life in perfection.

ॠ Ṝ is Śikhaṇḍi-Rūpa. Śikhaṇḍin is one of the Vidyeśvaras or lords of knowledge who administer Śiva's power of creation, maintenance and destruction in the world.

> The (Vidyeśvaras) are blue-black and red like blood, . .

. . dark like a cloud, (red) like kuṅkuma and (dark) like crushed khol.
The (Vidyeśvaras) have four arms and three eyes; they carry axe and trident (in their posterior hands) and make the gesture of bestowing and that of absence of fear (with their two other hands). They are dressed in linen and are immaculate.
Ananta, Sūkṣma, Śivotkṛṣṭa, and Ekanetraka, as well as Ekarudra, Trimūrti, Śrīkhaṇḍa, and Śikhaṇḍin: these are the eight Vidyeśvara who attend all sacrifices. Mayamatam 36:175-177.[4]

ॡ Lṛ and Lṝ are the two Aśvins. The Aśvins are twin gods of healing and medicine. The knowledge of Āyurvedic medicine came from Brahmā the creator, who first gave it to Prajāpati.

ब्रह्मणा हि यथाप्रोक्तमायुर्वेदं प्रजापतिः
जग्राह निखिलेनादावश्विनौ तु पुनस्ततः
अश्विभ्यां भगवाञ्छक्रः प्रतिपेदे ह केवलम्
ऋषिप्रोक्तो भरद्वाजस्तस्माच्छक्रमुपागमत् (Caraka Sū.1: 4-5)[5]

Prajāpati taught it to the Aśvins, and then the Aśvins gave it to Indra. Bharadvāja received the knowledge of Āyurveda from Indra, and taught it to the assembled sages: Thus the knowledge of Āyurveda came to mankind. The Aśvins symbolize the glow of sunrise appearing in the sky before the dawn, like a golden chariot, bringing treasures to men and averting misfortune and sickness. Nāsatya, "kind, helpful," is the name of one twin, and Dasra, "enlightened giving," is the name of the second. They are pictured as men with the heads of horses.

> The two Aśvins are seated on a lion throne and look like horses, they have the brilliance of dāḍimī flowers and they both wear sacrificial threads on each shoulder. Thus are to be represented these two healers. There are, too, a pair of female fan bearers, the one who is Mṛtsañjīvanī is shown in yellow and Viśalyakaraṇī is red and is to the rear. There are two women, one yellow, the other reddish. Dhanvantari and Ātreya are on the left; the one is yellow, the other red and both are dressed in black. Mayamatam 36: 167-170.[6]

ए E is Vīrabhadra. Vīrabhadra is a fierce warrior and general in the retinue of Lord Śiva. He is renowned for leading Śiva's hordes when they laid waste to the sacrificial ground during the sacrifice of Dakṣa—a sacrifice which was defective, because Lord Śiva, the Ruler of All, was not invited.

> Vīrabhadra is mounted on a bull and holds the trident (in one of his upper hands) and the mace (in the other); his two (lower hands) hold the viṇā or else make the gestures of absence of fear and bestowing, respectively. He has four arms and three eyes; his coiled hair is adorned with the crescent moon. He is provided with all jewels and is white and he has the bull for emblem. The god, seated on a lotiform seat, rests his back against a banyan. He is the Lord of the world, Śaṅkara, Śambhu, who is at the head of the Mothers. Mayamatam 36:213-215.[7]

ऐ AI is Vāgbhava, the essence or source of speech. The total power of expression in speech is encapsulated in the dipthong "ai", which starts with "a" the first sound of Ṛg Veda, and ends with "i", the last sound of Ṛg Veda, and thus contains within its range the total value of speech: In this way, "ai" is Vāgbhava, the essence or source or total range of expression in speech.

ओ O is Īśvara, the supreme God. Īśvara can refer either to Śiva or to Viṣṇu.

औ AU is Ādiśakti. Ādiśakti is the primeval creative power. It is called Māyā in Vedānta, and it is known as Durgā in the Purāṇas.

अं AṀ is Maheśa. Maheśa means "great ruler", and it is a name for Śiva.

> With his shaggy hair, shining like pure gold, with well fleshed thighs, (Maheśa) has hair which is stamped with the crescent moon with its intense rays; he has four arms and three eyes; he wears an amiable look and is in the prime of life; his chest is big and he is mounted on a bull. He carries a chain and an elephant hook and a noose. Muscled and wtih an arm raised, his hand like an elephant's trunk, he has a necklae and anklets as well as bracelets, hip girdle and ear-pendants in serpent form; his garment is a tiger skin, and his waist is clasped by a belt. Mayamatam 36: 35-38.[8]

अः AḤ is Kālarudra. Lord Śiva, becoming united with Kāla, time, creates this universe, and also destroys it. Rudra is the prime mover. Impelled by Rudra, Kāla, time, creates the universe and gives it momentum.

क KA is Prajāpati, Lord of created Beings. Prajāpati presides over the creation and protection of living beings. He is a single Creator, predating all the other gods. In the tenth mandala of Ṛg Veda, he is described: "He is the God of gods, and none beside him." In the Puruṣa Sūkta, Prajāpati is the original creative will which causes the projection of the universe in space and time.

ख KHA is Jāhnavī, the river Gaṅgā, personified in the goddess Gaṅgā. According to Bhāgavata Purāṇa, Lord Viṣṇu in one of his incarnations, appeared as the dwarf, Vāmana.

> In order to measure the universe in the court of Asura Mahābāli, he extended his left foot to the end of the universe and pierced a hole in its covering with the nail of his big toe. Through the hole, the pure water of the Causal Ocean entered this universe as the Ganges River. Having washed the lotus feet of the Lord, which are covered with reddish saffron, the water of the Ganges acquired a very beautiful pink colour. Because the Ganges directly touches the lotus feet of Lord Vishnu (Nārāyaṇa) before descending within this universe, Ganges is known as Bhāgavat-

Padī or Viṣṇupadī which means Emanating from the lotus feet of Bhagavan (God). It finally settles in Brahmaloka or Brahmapura, abode of Lord Brahmā before descending to planet Earth at the request of Bhagīratha and held safely by Lord Śiva on his head to prevent destruction of Bhūmi (Mother Earth). Then, the river Gangā was released from Lord Śiva 's hair to meet the needs of the country. To free the sons of Sagar, in another story, the Gangā flowed down into the nether regions, becoming the only river to flow through all the three worlds.[9]

The name Jāhnavī is explained in another story:

When Gangā came down to Earth, on her way to Bhagīratha, her rushing waters created turbulence and destroyed the fields and the sādhana of a sage called Jahnu. He was angered by this and drank up all of Gangā's waters. Upon this, the Gods prayed to Jahnu to release Gangā so that she could proceed on her mission. Pleased with their prayers, Jahnu released the waters of Gangā from his ears. Hence the name "Jāhnavi"(daughter of Jahnu) for Gangā.[10]

ग Ga is Gaṇapati, commonly known as Gaṇeśa. Gaṇeśa has the head of an elephant. He is called the Lord of Beginnings, and the Remover of Obstacles, and leader of all the classes of Beings (gaṇas). He is counted as one of the 5 Pañca Devatās, in which connection he is associated with Pṛthivī and the sense of smell.

He has an elephant's face and only one tusk; he is upright and holds himself to the right; he has three eyes, he is red; he has four arms and looks like a dwarf with a huge belly; a snake is his sacrificial thread. His thighs and knees are fat and heavy; he is seated on a lotiform throne with left leg stretched out and right bent. His trunk uncoils to the left. In one of his right hands he holds his broken tusk and, in the other, an elephant hook; the akṣa rosary should be in one of his left hands and a sweetmeat in the other. His hair is coiled into a tiara; he is adorned with necklaces and other jewels. This is Gaṇādhipa who may also be standing on a lotiform pedestal. When he is dancing he has six or four arms. The rat is his mount and his emblem. Mayamatam 36:122-126.[11]

घ GHA is Bhairava, a form of Śiva comprising all the three guṇas. He is described as being like pure crystal, effulgent as the rays of 1000 suns, shining like a sapphire thundercloud, and wearing sapphire colored clothing. He has three eyes, eight arms, has a fanged, fearsome gaping mouth, and a girdle and anklets of live serpents. He is Digambara, encompassing all the quarters, like space, and the prince-lord, Kumareśa. In his right hands he holds a staff with a skull on top, a sword, a noose and a trident. His left hands hold the damaru drum, a skull, the mudra bestowing boons, and a snake.[12]

ङ Ṅa is Kāla, Time personified. Kāla is the infinite, unbounded, world-destroying character of time, the ultimate and final administrator of all things. Thus Kāla is appreciated as the god of death and destruction, sometimes identified with Yama. In the Bhagavad Gītā, 11:32, Kṛṣṇa says,

> कालोऽस्मि लोकक्षयकृत्प्रवृद्धो लोकान्समाहर्तुमिह प्रवृत्तः
> I am Time, arisen with enormous stature for the destruction of the world, engaged here in unfolding the worlds.

च Ca is Caṇḍarudra, an aspect of Śiva. Caṇḍarudra is the brightly shining celestial glow at the junction point or gap between relative creation and absolute unmanifest pure Being.

> Caṇḍarudra is a beautiful red mixed with white. He has two arms, his hair is wreathed by leaves and he has śaṅkha and patra (types of earpendants); he wears a sacrificial thread, his clothing is white and he is immaculate.
> His hands are joined over his heart, an axe is between his arms, he sits on a semicircular seat and is adorned with a garland of flowers. He is adorned with all ornaments and has his hair braided or knotted in a coil. Mayamatam 36:186-188.[13]

छ Cha is Bhadrakālī. Bhadrakālī is a mother goddess, a gentle form of Durgā. The consort of Vīrabhadra, she is the supreme creativity. She wears a garland made of 50 human skulls, representing the 50 letters of the Sanskrit alphabet. She is one of the Divine Mothers attending on Skanda.

ज Ja is Jambhahā, the slayer of Jambha. Indra is the slayer of the demon Jambha: "Indra had in days of yore slain the Asura Jambha in the battle between the celestials and the Asuras." (MBh.7, 101, 17)[14]. Indra is the ever-victorious king of the gods, so this name for Indra emphasizes the quality of being victorious over all enemies.

झ Jha is Ardhanārīśa. Ardhanārīśa is the hermaphroditic form of Śiva as half-man and half-woman, symbolizing his transcendental wholeness in which opposites are bound together and integrated.

> The left half corresponds to Umā and the right to Īśa. (The right half) has hair in a matted coil of bright yellow with vivid decorations; the left half, that of Umā, has a dhammilla hair arrangement with curls and a parting and has a mark on the forehead. A pendant in the form of Vāsuki is arranged in the right ear and in the left, a tālika pendant or a pālika one.
>
> The two right hands hold the skull, or the trident, and the axe. The single left hand holds an utpala and (the corresponding arm) is adorned with armlet and bracelet. The sacrificial thread is aranged (on the) right (of the bust) and a rosary on the left. The left half of the neck wears a necklace and the right half is the color of fire. The half corresponding to Umā has a breast and the right half pectoral muscles. The right half of the waist wears a garment made of a tiger skin and the Umā half a hip girdle and a long garment in several colors.
>
> The two feet, that of the god and that of the goddess, rest

on the same lotus but the left leg, decorated with an anklet, is slightly bent; the left foot, that of the goddess, is decorated and wears rings. Mayamatam 36: 81-89.[15]

ञ Ña is Sarpa, the serpent devatā. The snake god rules the creative life-force and is the devatā of the Fine Arts. Connected with the nether-worlds, he protects treasures hidden in the earth. He has the power of transmutation, to transform something ugly and unformed into something beautiful, or to transform poison into nectar, ignorance into knowledge, or bondage into liberation.

ट Ṭa is Bhṛṅgīśa. Bhṛṅgīśa is the name of one of the commanders of the gaṇas in Gaṇapati's retinue. He was originally Andhaka, a demon who slew many devas and even challenged Lord Śiva. When he was impaled on Śiva's trident, he surrendered, and worshipped Lord Śiva. Śiva brought him back to life, gave him Divine powers of omniscience, and made him a general in Gaṇeśa's retinue.

ठ Ṭha is Candra, the Moon. The Moon is the lord of plants, the symbol of Soma, and also a symbol of beauty. In the 'Puruṣa Sūkta' of the Ṛg Veda it is mentioned that Candra was born from the mind of the Virāṭ Puruṣa.

Candra sits on a lion throne; he is (white) as a conch and

as jasmine. Encircled by a nimbus he has two arms and his face is white. Whether he is standing or seated his hands shine with the lotuses he holds. The strands of his sacrificial thread are gold. Soma is pleasant; he increases and decreases. He wears garlands and white clothing, is the color of gold and has red eyes. Mayamatam 36:157-159.[16]

ड Ḍa is Ekanetra. Ekanetra, "One-eyed," is one of the eight Vidyeśvaras, or lords of knowledge, who administer Śiva's power of creation, maintenance and destruction in the world.

The (Vidyeśvaras) are blue-black and red like blood, ... dark like a cloud, (red) like kuṅkuma and (dark) like crushed khol.
The (Vidyeśvaras) have four arms and three eyes; they carry axe and trident (in their posterior hands) and make the gesture of bestowing and that of absence of fear (with their two other hands). They are dressed in linen and are immaculate.
Ananta, Sūkṣma, Śivotkṛṣṭa, and Ekanetraka, as well as Ekarudra, Trimūrti, Śrīkhaṇḍa, and Śikhaṇḍin: these are the eight Vidyeśvara who attend all sacrifices. Mayamatam 36:175-177.[17]

ढ Ḍha is Yama. Yama is the supreme administrator, the ruler of death. Yama is depicted with blue skin and red clothes and rides a water buffalo. He holds a loop of rope in his left hand with which he lassoes souls.[18] In the Ṛg Veda he is mentioned as the son of Vivasvat and of Saraṇyū, the daughter of Tvaṣṭṛ, with a twin sister named Yamī.

> He who holds the mace in one hand and the noose in the other has eyes like dazzling fire. Mounted on a big buffalo, he is the color of khol and he shines.
> He is surrounded by his henchmen who resemble him; they have muscled chests and they are divine; these are the 'catchers' who are extremely strong, they stand at the door and are cruel, since they spread fear throughout the worlds. . . . Yama must be seated and he has the buffalo as emblem and mount. Mayamatam 36:144-149.[19]

ण Ṇa is Nandi. Nandi is the bull, the blessed companion and vehicle of Lord Śiva. He is the gate-keeper who controls access to Lord Śiva and his abode. He is said to represent the mind or soul that is completely dedicated to the Absolute, Lord Śiva.

त Ta is Vāstu Daivatya. Vāstu is the principle of architectural design which connects the individual expression of Natural Law with the intelligence of the cosmos. When the organization of space and form in the layout of houses, towns, cities, gardens, roads, water works, shops and public areas is completely in accordance with Total Natural Law, so that moving about in those structures the individual enjoys complete support of Natural Law, then that structure, form or space exhibits the quality of Vāstu. Vāstu is that intelligence of Nature which spontaneously computes perfection in the field of action through alignment with Total Natural Law on the material level.

थ Tha is Brahman. Brahman is the supreme realization, the goal of Vedānta, the highest attainment. It is Total Knowledge and Total Organizing Power, life in perfection.

द Da is the goddess Durgā. Durgā is the wife of Śiva, the mother of the universe. Durgā incarnated as the united power of all divine beings, who offered her the required physical attributes and weapons to kill the demon "Mahīṣāsura." She is depicted as having eight or ten hands representing the quadrants, three eyes, and rides on a lion. In her hands are conch, bow and arrow, thunderbolt, lotus, discus, sword and trident. She is one of the three main aspects of Mother Divine, with Lakṣmī and Sarasvatī.

ध Dha is Dhanada, wealth bestowing. Dhanada is a name of Lakṣmi, emphasizing her quality of bestowing wealth.

न Na is Sāvitrī. Sāvitrī is the life-giving, vivifying power of the sun. Savitṛ has golden arms, and is beautiful-handed. He is also pleasant tongued and iron-jawed. His eyes are golden as well. He is yellow-haired, and he puts on a tawny garment. He has a golden car with a golden pole, which is omni-form, just as he himself is capable of assuming all forms. His car is drawn by two radiant steeds or by two or more brown, white-footed horses. Mighty splendour ("amati") is preeminently attributed to Savitṛ, and mighty "golden" splendour to him only. Such splendour he stretches out or diffuses. He illumines the air, heaven and earth, the world, the spaces of the earth, and the vault of heaven.[20] Ṛg Veda 3.62.10-12 says:

> 10. We meditate on that desirable light of the divine Sāvitrī, who influences our pious rites.
> 11. Desirous with food, we solicit with praise, of the divine Sāvitrī, the gift of affluence.
> 12. Devout and wise men, impelled by intelligence, adore the divine Savitrī with sacrifices and sacred hymns.[21]

प Pa is Parjanya, the god of rain. The Bhagavad Gītā, Ch. 3 v.14 says, "From food creatures come into being; from rain (Parjanya) is produced food."[22] Living beings are created and find their source in food, and food is created by rainfall. Parjanya gives us the material blessings of rainfall and thus abundance in the material world by the creation of food and other crops.[23] Ṛg Veda V.83 celebrates Parjanya, the god of rain, as follows:

> 1. I address the mighty Parjanya who is present: Praise him with these hymns; worship him with reverence, him who

is the thunderer, the showerer, the bountiful, who impregnates the plants with rain.
2. He strikes down the trees, he destroys the Rākṣasas, he terrifies the whole world by his mighty weapon: even the innocent man flies from the sender of rain, when Parjanya, thundering, slays the wicked.
3. As a charioteer, urging his horses with his whip, brings into view the messenger (of war), so Parjanya, (driving the clouds before him), makes manifest the messengers of the rain: the roaring of the lion-(like cloud) proclaims from afar that Parjanya overspreads the sky with rainy clouds.
4. The winds blow strong, the lightnings flash, the plants spring up, the firmament dissolves: earth becomes (fit) for all creatures when Parjanya fertilizes the soil with showers.
5. Do thou, Parjanya, through whose function the earth is bowed down; through whose function hoofed cattle thrive; through whose function plants assume all kinds of forms, grant us great felicity.
6. Send down for us, Maruts, the rain from heaven: drops of the rainy charger descend: come down Parjanya, sprinkling water by this thundering (cloud); thou who art the sender of rain, our protector.
7. Cry aloud over (the earth); thunder; impregnate the plants; traverse (the sky) with thy water-laden chariot, draw open the tight-fastened, downward-turned water bag, and may the high and low places be made level.
8. Raise on high the mighty sheath (of rain), pour down (its contents); let the rivers flow unimpeded to the east; saturate with water both heaven and earth, and let there be abundant beverage for the kine.
9. When, Parjanya, sounding loud and thundering, thou destroyest the wicked (clouds), this whole (world) rejoices,

and all that is upon the earth.
10. Thou hast rained: now check well the rain: thou has made the deserts capable of being crossed: thou has given birth to plants for (man's) enjoyment: verily thou hast obtained laudation from the people.[24]

फ Pha is Paśupati. Paśupati is an incarnation of Lord Śiva as lord of animals. Paśupati has five faces, Sadyojata, Vāmadeva, Tatpuruṣa, Aghora and Īśana, representing the 5 elements. The 12 Jyotir Liṅgas in India are the body and the Jyotirliṅga at Pāśupatināth temple in Kathmandu, Nepal, is the head over the body. The Paśupatināth temple housing the Jyotirliṅgam tells this story[25]:

> Śiva and Parvati came to the Kathmandu Valley and rested by the Bagmatī while on a journey. Shiva was so impressed by its beauty and the surrounding forest that he and Parvati changed themselves into deer and walked into the forest. Many spots in the Kathmandu Valley are identified as places where Śiva went during his time as a deer. After a while the people and gods began to search for Śiva. Finally, they found him in the forest, but he refused to leave. Ultimately Śiva announced that, since he had lived by the Bagmatī River in a deer's form, he would now be known as Paśupatināth, Lord of all animals. It is said that whoever came here and beheld the liṅgam that appeared there would not be reborn as an animal.

ब Ba is Trimūrti. Trimūrti, “embodying three,” is one of the Vidyeśvaras, or lords of knowledge, who administer Śiva's power of creation, maintenance and destruction in the world.

> The (Vidyeśvaras) are blue-black and red like blood, ... dark like a cloud, (red) like kuṅkuma and (dark) like crushed khol.
> The (Vidyeśvaras) have four arms and three eyes; they carry axe and trident (in their posterior hands) and make the gesture of bestowing and that of absence of fear (with their two other hands). They are dressed in linen and are immaculate.
> Ananta, Sūkṣma, Śivotkṛṣṭa, and Ekanetraka, as well as Ekarudra, Trimūrti, Śrīkhaṇḍa, and Śikhaṇḍin: these are the eight Vidyeśvara who attend all sacrifices. Mayamatam 36:175-177.[26]

भ Bha is Bhārgava. Bhṛgu is one of the seven Divine Ṛṣis. Bhārgava means descendent of the Ṛṣi Bhṛgu. By some accounts, the eleven Rudras are descendants of Bhṛgu. They are Ajaikapāt, Ahirbudhnya, Virūpākṣa, Sureśvara, Jayanta, Bahurūpa, Aparājita, Sāvitra, Tryaṁbaka, Vaivasvata and Hara. These are organizing powers in the gap between relative and absolute that are responsible for connecting the eternal, immortal field of Being with the ever-changing field of relativity, by upholding and preserving coherence, balance, stability and eternal order in the process of manifestation. According to Vāruṇa Purāṇa, Śiva created the eleven Rudras in order to help Brahmā create creation, and they are responsible for the evolutionary flow of beings in creation. Mayamatam says the eleven rudra resemble a furious fire (36:175).[27]

म Ma is Madana, "intoxicating," a name of Kāmadeva, the god of love. Kāmadeva is represented as a young, handsome winged man with green skin who wields a bow and arrows. His bow is made of sugarcane with a string of honeybees, and his arrows are decorated with five kinds of fragrant flowers. The five flowers are Aśoka tree flowers, white and blue lotus flowers, Mallika plant (Jasmine) and Mango tree flowers.[28]

> Kāma is gold colored and adorned with all jewels; he has two arms; his appearance is charming and pleasant and he is all yellow. Whether on a throne or in a chariot, he illumines all the worlds. . . . His sugarcane bow and his five arrows—one that scorches people, one that sets on fire, one that deludes all people, one that crushes all people, and one that kills—are to be placed in the west. Such is Smara to be, whose emblem is the Makara. Mayamatam 36:162-167.[29]

य Ya is Vāyu devatā, the lord of the winds. Vāyu is the air element, one of the five pañcamahābhūtas. The Bṛhadāraṇyaka describes how the gods once engaged in a contest to determine who among them is the greatest. When a deity such as that of vision would leave a man's body, that man would continue to live, albeit as a blind man. He regained the lost faculty once the errant deity returned to his post. One by one the deities all took their turns leaving the body, but the man continued to live on, though impaired in various ways. Finally, when Vāyu started to leave the body, all the other deities started to be ripped out of the body with him, "just as a powerful horse yanks off pegs in the ground to which he is bound." This caused the other deities to realize that they can function only when empowered by Vāyu. Then they honored Vāyu and made offerings to him.[30] Vāyu is celebrated in many Ṛg Vedic hymns, including this one, 10.168 [31]:

> 1. (I proclaim) the greatness of the impetuous Vāyu; his voice spreads thundering around; he moves along sweeping the sky, tinting purple (the quarters of the horizon), he advances, raising the dust of the earth.
> 2. Solid masses advance to meet the wind; the mares come to him as to battle; associated with them and in the same car the divinity proceeds, the sovereign of all this world.
> 3. Traversing the firmament by its paths, (Vāyu) rests not for a single day: the friend of the waters, the first-born, the utterer of truth—where has he been generated, whence was he manifested?
> 4. The soul of the gods, the germ of the world, this divinity moves according to his pleasure; his voices are heard, his form is not (seen); let us worship that Vāta with oblations.

Mayamatam describes Vāyu as follows:

> He with the flag in his hand is very strong, his eyes are red and he is a smoky color; Vāyu has arched eyebrows and he is clothed in motley colors. He rides a gazelle and is to be

installed with ornaments. Mayamatam 36:153-154. [32]

र Ra is Vahni Devatā, the devatā of conveyances. Vahni Devatā is Agni, fire, because Agni is the conveyer (vahni) or bearer of oblations to the gods. Vahni is the first of the seven names of Agni. According to Mayamatam:

> Agni has the appearance of an old man; he stands upon a semicircular pedestal and shines like pure gold; his eyebrows and eyes are russet. He has a golden beard and hair of the same tone and wears a garment the color of the rising sun and a sacrificial thread in the same shade.
>
> In his right hand is a karaka pitcher and, in his left, an akṣa rosary. He has seven weapons and a form rendered brilliant by his curls and braids which are seven rays of light, glowing from his garland of fire and dazzling, he is surrounded by a nimbus of fire.
>
> He is mounted on a ram and is near a firepit and he must wear the ascetic's belt. Svāhā is to his right, adorned with jewelled ear rings. Agni, whose adornments are russet and who is favorable towards all sacrifices is pure. Mayamatam 36:139-143. [33]

ल La is Pṛthivī. Pṛthivī is the earth or wide world—'the broad and extended One,' personified as Devī. She is the subject matter of the first Sūkta of Book 12 of Atharva Veda[34]:

> 1. Truth, high and potent Law, the Consecrating Rite, Fervour, Brahma, and Sacrifice uphold the Earth. May she, the Queen of all that is and is to be, may Pṛthivī make

ample space and room for us.
2. Not over awed by the crowd of Manu's sons, she who hath many heights and floods and level plains; She who bears plants endowed with many varied powers, may Pṛthivī for us spread wide and favour us.
3. In whom the sea, and Sindhu, and the waters, in whom our food and corn-lands had their being, In whom this all that breathes and moves is active, this Earth assign us foremost rank and station!
4. She who is Lady of the earth's four regions, in whom our food and corn-lands had their being, Nurse in each place of breathing, moving creatures, this Earth, vouchsafe us kine with milk that fails not!
5. On whom the men of old before us battled, on whom the Gods attacked the hostile demons, The varied home of bird, and kine and horses, this Prithivī vouchsafe us luck and splendour!
6. Firm standing-place, all-bearing, store of treasures, gold-breasted, harbourer of all that moveth. May Earth who bears Agni Vaiśvānara, Consort of mighty Indra, give us great possessions.
7. May Earth, may Pṛthivī, always protected with ceaseless care by Gods who never slumber, May she pour out for us delicious nectar, may she bedew us with a flood of splendour.
8. She who at first was water in the ocean, whom with their wondrous powers the sages followed, May she whose heart is in the highest heaven, compassed about with truth, and everlasting, May she, this Earth, bestow upon us lustre, and grant us power in loftiest dominion.
9. On whom the running universal waters flow day and night with never-ceasing motion, May she with many

streams pour milk to feed us, may she bedew us with a flood of splendour.
10. She whom the Aśvins measured out, o'er whom the foot of Viṣṇu strode, Whom Indra, Lord of Power and Might, freed from all foemen for himself, May Earth pour out her milk for us, a mother unto me her son.
11. Pṛthivī, auspicious be thy woodlands, auspicious be thy hills and snow-clad mountains. Unslain, unwounded, unsubdued, I have set foot upon the Earth....

व Va is Varuṇa. Varuṇa is the devatā of the ocean, and the regent of the Western direction. In the Mahābhārata, the story is told of how Varuṇa came to be the Lord of the Waters:

> In Kṛtayuga, the Devas approached Varuṇa and said to him, "You must be the lord of all the waters, as Indra is our protector. You can live in the heart of the ocean. All the rivers in the world, and the ocean which is their husband will obey you. You will wax and wane along with Candra (moon)." Varuṇa agreed to comply with their request. All of them anointed Varuṇa as the King of the waters. (Śalya Parva, Chapter 47).[35]

Mayamatam says:

> He who holds the noose in his hand, is white as the moon, as jasmine, as shells, and he is very strong. Adorned with two sorts of gold ear-rings as well as with necklaces and armlets, he wears yellow raiment, is incomparable, is golden in color and nothing but joy. Whether seated or standing, Varuṇa must be on a makara. Mayamatam 36: 152.[36]

श Śa is Lakṣmī. Lakṣmī is Mother Divine, the consort of Viṣṇu, the goddess of light, wealth, prosperity, and fortune, and the embodiment of beauty, grace and charm. Her four hands represent the four goals of human life, dharma, artha, kāma and mokṣa (duty, wealth, fulfillment of desire, and liberation). Lakṣmī sprang from the ocean of milk when it was churned by the gods and demons for the sake of the Amṛta. Wealth, both spiritual and material flows out of her hands. Lakṣmī is the power of Viṣṇu, and the personification of spiritual fulfillment.

> Lakṣmi is seated on a lotus, she has two arms; she is golden and shines with gold and jewels; one of her ear-pendants is in makara form whilst the other is in the form of a conch. She is a beautiful, accomplished young woman whose limbs are harmonious and who plays with her arched eyebrows. Her figure is rounded; she has karṇapūra and her eyes are like lotuses; her lips are red, her cheeks plump and her breast covered with a bodice. Lotus, parting, conch and discus are her head ornaments. It is prescribed that a lotus be placed in her right hand and the Śrīphala in her left. Her beautiful breasts and large hips are covered with a fine garment; she wears a waist girdle and a hip girdle. Her hair is arranged in a tiara and she is sitting in lotus posture. Mayamatam 36: 247-252.[37]

ष Ṣa is Dvādaśātmā, the Ātmā or transcendental Self, that is represented by the 12 Jyotir Liṅgas of India. The Jyotir Liṅgas are manifest representations of the infinitely extended Liṅgam or pillar of light, which is the visible sign of the supreme, Brahman. The vision or Darśan of the infinite pillar of light is said to be the culminating experience of God Consciousness, and the first step of the awakening of totality on the path to Brahman Consciousness, as described in the Brahma Sūtra, the textbook of Vedānta. It is this lofty experience of higher consciousness on the threshold of Unity that is the Ātmā or transcendental essence of the twelve Jyotirliṅgas.

स Sa is Śakti. Śakti is the primordial cosmic energy. It is the dynamism of Total Natural Law, the organizing power at the basis of creation, the agent of all change. Śakti is the personification of the Divine feminine creative power, the consort of Lord Śiva. There are 64 Śakti Pīṭha, shrines scattered throughout India where Mother Divine in the form of Satī, Parvatī or Durgā is especially lively.

ह Ha is Śiva, eternal peace, the transcendental fourth state of consciousness: The Upanishads proclaim:

शिवं शान्तमद्वैतं चतुर्थं मन्यन्ते स आत्मा स विज्ञेयः

Śivaṁ śāntam advaitaṁ caturthaṁ manyante, sa ātmā, sa vijñeyaḥ—Nṛsiṁhottaratāpanī Upaniṣad

"Śiva is peace, the transcendental fourth state of consciousness, He is the Self, He is worth knowing." Śiva is depicted with the crescent moon on his head, and with the river Gaṅgā falling on his head and flowing downward in three directions. He has a third eye on his forehead, and his matted hair is tied by a string of Rudrākṣa beads. A great cobra is coiled around his neck, and his water pot and trident are close by Him.

ळ Ḷa is Ātmā, the pure Self, infinite, unbounded and unmanifest.

Observations about the Devatās of the Letters

Nine letters have alliterative devatās, i.e. devatās that begin with the same letter.

Table of Letters with Alliterative Devatās			
Ga	Gaṇapati	Ca	Caṇḍarudra
Ja	Jambhahā	Da	Durgā
Dha	Dhanada	Pa	Parjanya
Bha	Bhārgava	Ma	Madana
Va	Varuṇa		

There are three "twin" letters, letters which share the same devatā:

Table of Twin Letters with Same Devatā		
Ṛ	Tha	Brahman
U	Ta	Vāstu devatā
Lṛ	Lṝ	Aśvins

There are nine letters representing Mother Divine:

Table of Letters of Mother Divine			
Ā	Parāśakti	Ī	Māyāśakti
Au	Ādiśakti	Kha	Jāhnavī (Mother Gaṅgā)
Cha	Bhadrakālī	Da	Durgā
La	Pṛthivī (Mother Earth)	Śa	Lakṣmī
Sa	Śakti		

Notes

1. Dagens, Bruno, tr., *Mayamatam: Treatise of Housing, Architecture and Iconography*, Motilal Banarsidass: Delhi, 2007. ISBN 81-2081226-3.
2. T.A.G. Rao, *Elements of Hindu Iconography*, Motilal Banarsidass: Delhi, January 1997. ISBN 81-208-0876-2.
3. Dagens, op. cit.
4. Ibid.
5. Story from beginning of Caraka Saṁhitā: See for example Sharma, P., *Caraka-Saṁhitā, Agniveśa's treatise refined and annotated by Caraka and redacted by Dṛḍhabala, Text with English Translation*, Chaukhambha Orientalia, Varanasi: 1981, vol. 1, p.3.
6. Dagens, op. cit.
7. Ibid.
8. Ibid.
9. Wikipedia article on Ganges: https://en.wikipedia.org/wiki/Ganges_in_Hinduism
10. Ibid.
11. Dagens, op. cit.
12. Article on "Shri Bhairava Deva," www.shivashakti.com/bhairava.htm.
13. Dagens, op. cit.
14. Ganguli, Kisari Mohan, *The Mahabharata of Krishna-Dwaipayana Vyasa, Translated into English Prose from the original Sanskrit Text*, Munshiram

Manoharlal, New Delhi: 1976, Vol. VI, Drona Parva, p. 205.
15. Dagens, Bruno, op. cit.
16. Ibid.
17. Ibid.
18. Wikipedia article on Yama: https://en.wikipedia.org/wiki/Yama
19. Dagens, op. cit.
20. Wikipedia article on Savitr: https://en.wikipedia.org/wiki/Savitr
21. Wilson, H.H., *Ṛgveda Saṁhitā*, Nag Publishers, Delhi: 1990.
22. Maharishi Mahesh Yogi, *On the Bhagavad Gita, Chapters 1–6*, Penguin Books, 1990.
23. Wikipedia article on Parjanya, https://en.wikipedia.org/wiki/Parjanya
24. Wilson, *Ṛgveda Saṁhitā*, op. cit.
25. Wikipedia article on Pashupatinath Temple in Nepal: https://en.wikipedia.org/wiki/Pashupatinath_Temple
26. Dagens, op. cit.
27. Ibid.
28. Wikipedia article on Kāmadeva: https://en.wikipedia.org/wiki/Kamadeva
29. Dagens, op. cit.
30. Wikipedia article on Vāyu: https://en.wikipedia.org/wiki/Vayu.

31. Wilson, *Ṛgveda Saṁhitā*, op. cit.
32. Dagens, op. cit.
33. Ibid.
34. Griffith, R.T.H., *The Hymns of the Atharvaveda, Volume 2*, Rarebooksclub.com reprint of 1895 edition.
35. Mani, Vettam, *Purāṇic Encyclopedia: a comprehensive dictionary with special reference to the epic and Puranic literature*, Motilal Banarsidass: Delhi, 1975.
36. Dagens, op. cit.
37. Ibid.

Varṇa	Letter	Gender	Quality	Color	Devatā	Boon
अ	a	masc.	rajas	red	All Devatās	
आ	ā	fem.	sattva	white	Parāśakti	
इ	i	masc.	tamas	black	Viṣṇu	
ई	ī	fem.	rajas	yellow	Māyā Śakti	
उ	u	masc.	tamas	black	Vāstu Devatā	
ऊ	ū	fem.	tamas	black	Bhūmi	
ऋ	ṛ	neuter	rajas	yellow	Brahman	
ॠ	ṝ	neuter	rajas	yellow	Śikhaṇḍirūpa	
ऌ	lṛ	neuter	rajas	red	Aśvins	
ॡ	lṝ	neuter	rajas	red	Aśvins	
ए	e	masc.	rajas	yellow	Vīrabhadra	granting siddhis
ऐ	ai	fem.	sattva	white	Vāgbhava	
ओ	o	masc.	sattva	white	Īśvara	bestowing fruit
औ	au	fem.	sattva	white	Ādiśakti	granting success in all things
अं	aṁ	masc.	rajas	red	Maheśa	
अः	aḥ	fem.	rajas	red	Kālarudra	

Varṇa	Letter	Gender	Quality	Color	Devatā	Boon
क	ka	masc.	rajas	yellow	Prajāpati	bestowing rain
ख	kha	fem.	sattva	milk-white	Jāhnavī	destroying sin
ग	ga	masc.	rajas	red	Gaṇapati	eliminating obstacles
घ	gha	fem.	sattva	pearl-white	Bhairava	destroying enemies
ङ	ṅa	neuter	tamas	black	Kāla	overcoming death
च	ca	masc.	tamas	collyrium	Caṇḍarudra	
छ	cha	fem.	tamas	black	Bhadrakālī	bringing fame
ज	ja	masc.	rajas	red	Jambhahā (Indra)	bringing victory
झ	jha	fem.	tamas	mixed red and black	Ardhanārīśa	
ञ	ña	neuter	rajas	yellow	Sarpa Devatā	
ट	ṭa	masc.	rajas	red	Bhṛṅgīśa	
ठ	ṭha	fem.	sattva	white	Candra (Moon)	
ड	ḍa	masc.	rajas	yellow	Ekanetra	
ढ	ḍha	fem.	tamas	indigo blue	Yama	destroying death

Varṇa	Letter	Gender	Quality	Color	Devatā	Boon
ण	ṇa	neuter	rajas	red	Nandi	granting achievement of the goal
त	ta	masc.	sattva	white	Vāstu Devatā	
थ	tha	fem.	sattva	white	Brahman	
द	da	masc.	tamas	black	Durgā	granting success
ध	dha	fem.	rajas	yellow	Dhanada	granting achievement of the goal
न	na	neuter	sattva	crystalline	Sāvitrī	destroying sin
प	pa	masc.	sattva	white	Parjanya	granting perfection in rain
फ	pha	fem.	sattva	white	Paśupati	destroying sin
ब	ba	masc.	rajas	yellow	Trimūrti	granting success in all things
भ	bha	fem.	rajas	red	Bhārgava	bestowing good fortune
म	ma	neuter	tamas	black	Madana	bestowing the fruit of all desires
य	ya	neuter	tamas	black	Vāyu	destroying enemies
र	ra	neuter	rajas	red	Vahni	
ल	la	neuter	rajas	yellow	Pṛthivī	supporting procurement

Varṇa	Letter	Gender	Quality	Color	Devatā	Boon
व	va	neuter	sattva	white	Varuṇa	destroying boundaries
श	śa	fem.	rajas	gold	Lakṣmī	
ष	ṣa	masc.	rajas	red	Dvādaśātmā	bestowing victory
स	sa	fem.	rajas	red	Śakti	creating stability
ह	ha	neuter	sattva	pure crystalline white	Śiva	granting eight siddhis, enjoyment and liberation
ळ	ḷa	neuter	rajas	red	Ātmā	granting success in all things

वर्णशिक्षा

वर्णानां स्त्रीपुंनपुंसकसंज्ञा

varṇānāṁ strī-puṁ-napuṁsaka-saṁjñā

ककारं च गकारं च चकारं च जकारकम्
टकारं च डकारं च तकारं च दकारकम् १

1. kakāraṁ ca gakāraṁ ca cakāraṁ ca jakārakam
ṭakāraṁ ca ḍakāraṁ ca takāraṁ ca dakārakam

पकारं च बकारं च षकारं च क्षकारकम्
एते द्वादशवर्णाः स्युः पुंल्लिङ्गाश्चेति कीर्तिताः २

2. pakāraṁ ca bakāraṁ ca ṣakāraṁ ca kṣakārakam
ete dvādaśa varṇāḥ syuḥ puṁlliṅgāś ceti kīrtitāḥ

खकारं च घकारं च छकारं च झकारकम्
ठकारं च ढकारं च थकारं च धकारकम् ३

3. khakāraṁ ca ghakāraṁ ca chakāraṁ ca jhakārakam
ṭhakāraṁ ca ḍhakāraṁ ca thakāraṁ ca dhakārakam 3

फकारं च भकारं च शकारं च सकारकम्
एते वै भानुबीजानि जायाश्चेति प्रकीर्तिताः ४

4. phakāraṁ ca bhakāraṁ ca śakāraṁ ca sakārakam
ete vai bhānu-bījāni jāyāś ceti prakīrtitāḥ

शेषं नपुंसकं ज्ञेयं त्रयो भेदा इति स्मृताः ५

5. śeṣaṁ napuṁsakaṁ jñeyaṁ trayo bhedā iti smṛtāḥ

शिवाग्निभूतरुद्राश्च त्रयोदश तिथिस्तथा
एते वै स्वरवर्णाः स्युः पुंल्लिङ्गाश्चेति कीर्तिताः ६

6. śivāgni-bhūta-rudrāś ca trayodaśa tithis tathā
ete vai svara-varṇāḥ syuḥ puṁlliṅgāś ceti kīrtitāḥ

पक्षो वेदरसा भानुर्मनुशैवाधिकारकाः
एतानि स्वरवर्णानि स्त्रीलिङ्गानीति कीर्त्यते ७

7. pakṣo veda-rasā bhānur manu-śaivādhikārakāḥ
etāni svara-varṇāni strī-liṅgānīti kīrtyate

प्रकृतिः सप्तवर्णानि विकृतिस्तु नवार्णकम्
प्रकृतिर्ह्रस्वमित्युक्तं विकृतिर्दीर्घमुच्यते ८

8. prakṛtiḥ saptavarṇāni vikṛtis tu navārṇakam
prakṛtir hrasvam ity uktaṁ vikṛtir dīrgham ucyate

प्रथमाश्च तृतीयाश्च षकारश्च क्षकारकम्
एते द्वादशवर्णाः स्युः पुंल्लिङ्गाश्चेति कीर्तिताः ९

9. prathamāś ca tṛtīyāś ca ṣakāraś ca kṣakārakam
ete dvādaśa varṇāḥ syuḥ puṁlliṅgāś ceti kīrtitāḥ

द्वितीयाश्च चतुर्थाश्च शसकारौ तथैव च
एते द्वादशवर्णाः स्युः स्त्रील्लिङ्गाश्चेति प्रकीर्तिताः १०

10. dvitīyāś ca caturthāś ca śasakārau tathaiva ca
ete dvādaśa varṇāḥ syuḥ strī-lliṅgāś ceti prakīrtitāḥ

अन्तस्थाश्चोत्तमाश्चैव ॠ ॡ वर्णौ तथैव च

हकारश्च ळकारश्च क्लीबाश्चेति प्रकीर्तिताः ११

11. antasthāś cottamāś caiva ṛ lṛ varṇau tathaiva ca
hakāraś ca ḷakāraś ca klībāś ceti prakīrtitāḥ

वर्णानां सत्वरजस्तमो गुणाः

varṇānāṁ satva-rajas-tamo guṇāḥ

पक्षो गृहार्थसंख्या च त्रयोदशमनुस्तथा
एते वै सात्विकगुणाः श्वेतवर्णं तथैव च १२

12. pakṣo gṛhārtha-saṁkhyā ca trayodaśa manus tathā
ete vai sātvika-guṇāḥ śveta-varṇaṁ tathaiva ca

शिवाब्धिसप्तावसुदिक्च रुद्राः तिथिश्चैव कलास्तथा
एते वै राजसगुणा रक्तवर्णं तथैव च १३

13. śivābdhi-saptā-vasu-dik ca rudrāḥ tithiś caiva kalās tathā
ete vai rājasa-guṇā rakta-varṇaṁ tathaiva ca

बाणो रसस्तृतीया च श्यामवर्णं तमो गुणः
हल् द्वितीया च चतुर्थश्च तवर्गप्रथमोत्तमौ १४

14. bāṇo rasas tṛtīyā ca śyāma-varṇaṁ tamo guṇaḥ
hal dvitīyā ca caturthaś ca tavarga-prathamottamau

पवर्गप्रथमश्चैव वेदाष्टादश एव च
एते वै सात्विकगुणाः श्वेतवर्णं तथैव च १५

15. pavarga-prathamaś caiva vedāṣṭādaśa eva ca
ete vai sātvika-guṇāḥ śveta-varṇaṁ tathaiva ca

खकारं च घकारं च ठकारं च थकारकम्
तकारं च नकारं च पकारं च फकारकम्
वकारं च हकारश्च क्षकारं चेति सात्त्विकः १६

16. khakāraṁ ca ghakāraṁ ca ṭhakāraṁ ca thakārakam
takāraṁ ca nakāraṁ ca pakāraṁ ca phakārakam
vakāraṁ ca hakāraś ca kṣakāraṁ ceti sātvikaḥ

कवर्गप्रथमश्चैव टवर्गश्च तथैव च
तृतीयाश्च तपवर्गचतुर्थाश्च चटवर्गोत्तमौ तथा १७

17. kavarga-prathamaś caiva ṭavargaś ca tathaiva ca
tṛtīyāś ca ta-pa-varga-caturthāś ca ca-ṭa-vargottamau tathā

ऊष्माणश्चैव रेफश्च लळकारौ रजोगुणाः
कवर्गप्रथमश्चैव टवर्गश्च तथैव च १८

18. ūṣmāṇaś caiva rephaś ca laḷakārau rajo-guṇāḥ
kavarga-prathamaś caiva ṭavargaś ca tathaiva ca

तृतीयाश्च भकारश्च धकारं च ञकारकम्
णकारं चोष्मणश्चैव रेफश्चैव लळौ तथा
एते रजोगुणाः प्रोक्ता रक्तवर्णं तथैव च १९

19. tṛtīyāś ca bhakāraś ca dhakāraṁ ca ñakārakam
ṇakāraṁ coṣmaṇaś caiva rephaś caiva laḷau tathā
ete rajo-guṇāḥ proktā rakta-varṇaṁ tathaiva ca

चकारश्च द्वितीया च ङकारं च मकारकम् २०

20. cakāraś ca dvitīyā ca ṅakāraṁ ca makārakam

ढकारं च दकारं च यकारं च झकारकम्

तामसः कृष्णवर्णं च उत्तमश्च मिश्रकम् २१

21. ḍhakāraṁ ca dakāraṁ ca yakāraṁ ca jhakārakam
tāmasaḥ kṛṣṇa-varṇaṁ ca uttamaś ca miśrakam

चकारश्च द्वितीया च आद्यन्तौ वर्गपञ्चमौ

चटवर्गचतुर्थौ च तवर्गश्च तृतीयकम् २२

22. cakāraś ca dvitīyā ca ādyantau varga-pañcamau
ca-ṭa-varga-caturthau ca ta-vargaś ca tṛtīyakam

यकारस्तामसगुणः श्यामवर्णस्तथैव च २३

23. yakāras tāmasa-guṇaḥ śyāma-varṇas tathaiva ca

अकारं सर्वदैवत्यं रक्तवर्णं रजः स्मृतम्

आकारः स्यात्पराशक्तिः श्वेतं सात्विकमुच्यते २४

24. akāraṁ sarva-daivatyaṁ raktavarṇaṁ rajaḥ smṛtam
ākāraḥ syāt parāśaktiḥ śvetaṁ sātvikam ucyate

इकारं विष्णुदैवत्यं श्यामं तामसमुच्यते

मायाशक्तिरितीकारं पीतं राजसमुच्यते २५

25. ikāraṁ viṣṇu-daivatyaṁ śyāmaṁ tāmasam ucyate
māyāśaktir itīkāraṁ pītaṁ rājasam ucyate

उकारं वास्तुदैवत्यं कृष्णं तामसमीरितम्

ऊकारं भूमिदैवत्यं श्यामळं तामसं भवेत् २६

26. ukāraṁ vāstu-daivatyaṁ kṛṣṇaṁ tāmasam īritam
ūkāraṁ bhūmi-daivatyaṁ śyāmaḷaṁ tāmasaṁ bhavet

ऋकारं ब्रह्मणो ज्ञेयं पीतं राजसमुच्यते
शिखण्डिरूपं ॠकारं राजसं पीतवर्णकम् २७

27. ṛkāraṁ brahmaṇo jñeyaṁ pītaṁ rājasam ucyate
śikhaṇḍi-rūpaṁ ṝkāraṁ rājasaṁ pīta-varṇakam

अश्विनौ तु ऌ ॡ प्रोक्तौ
एकारं वीरभद्रं स्याद्रजः पीतं तु सिद्धिदम् २८

28. aśvinau tu ḷṛ ḷṝ proktau
ekāraṁ vīrabhadraṁ syād rajaḥ pītaṁ tu siddhidam

ऐकारं वाग्भवं विन्द्यात्
ओकारमीश्वरं विन्द्याज्ज्योतिः सत्वं फलप्रदम् २९

29. aikāraṁ vāg-bhavaṁ vindyāt
okāram īśvaraṁ vindyāj jyotiḥ satvaṁ phala-pradam

औकारमादिशक्तिः स्याच्छुक्लं सर्वत्र सिद्धिदम्
अंकारं तु महेशं स्याद्रक्तवर्णं तु राजसम् ३०

30. aukāram ādiśaktiḥ syāc chuklaṁ sarvatra siddhidam
aṁkāraṁ tu maheśaṁ syād raktavarṇaṁ tu rājasam

अःकारं कालरुद्रं च रक्तं राजसमुच्यते
प्राजापत्यं ककारं स्यात्पीतं वृष्टिप्रदं रजः ३१

31. aḥkāraṁ kālarudraṁ ca raktaṁ rājasam ucyate
prājāpatyaṁ kakāraṁ syāt pītaṁ vṛṣṭi-pradaṁ rajaḥ

खकारं जाह्नवीबीजं क्षीराभं पापनाशनम्

गाणपत्यं गकारं स्याद्रक्ताभं विघ्ननाशनम् ३२

32. khakāraṁ jāhnavī-bījaṁ kṣīrābhaṁ pāpa-nāśanam

gāṇapatyaṁ gakāraṁ syād raktābhaṁ vighna-nāśanam

घकारं भैरवं ज्ञेयं मुक्ताभं शत्रुनाशनम्

ङकारं कालबीजं स्यात्कालं तार्क्ष्यं समुच्यते ३३

33. ghakāraṁ bhairavaṁ jñeyaṁ muktābhaṁ śatru-nāśanam

ṅakāraṁ kāla-bījaṁ syāt kālaṁ tārkṣyaṁ samucyate

चकारं चण्डरुद्रं स्यात् अञ्जनाभं तु तामसम्

छकारं भद्रकाळी स्यात्तामसं परिकीर्तितम् ३४

34. cakāraṁ caṇḍa-rudraṁ syāt añjanābhaṁ tu tāmasam

chakāraṁ bhadrakāḷī syāt tāmasaṁ parikīrtitam

जकारं जम्भहा ज्ञेयं रक्ताभं च जयावहम्

झकारमर्धनारीशं श्यामरक्तं तु मिश्रकम् ३५

35. jakāraṁ jambhahā jñeyaṁ raktābhaṁ ca jayāvaham

jhakāram ardha-nārīśaṁ śyāmaraktaṁ tu miśrakam

ञकारं सर्पदैवत्यं पीतं राजसरूपकम्

भृङ्गीशं स्याट्टकारं तु रक्तं राजसमेव च ३६

36. ñakāraṁ sarpa-daivatyaṁ pītaṁ rājasa-rūpakam

bhṛṅgīśaṁ syāṭ ṭakāraṁ tu raktaṁ rājasam eva ca

ठकारं चन्द्रबीजं स्याच्छ्वेतं सात्त्विकमुच्यते
डकारं चैकनेत्रं स्यात्पीतं राजसमुच्यते ३७

37. ṭhakāraṁ candra-bījaṁ syāc chvetaṁ sātvikam ucyate
ḍakāraṁ caika-netraṁ syāt pītaṁ rājasam ucyate 37

ढकारं यमबीजं स्यान्नीलं मृत्युविनाशनम्
णकारं नन्दिबीजं स्याद्रक्ताभं चार्थसिद्धिदम् ३८

38. ḍhakāraṁ yama-bījaṁ syān nīlaṁ mṛtyu-vināśanam
ṇakāraṁ nandi-bījaṁ syād raktābhaṁ cārtha-siddhidam

तकारं वास्तुदैवत्यं श्वेतं
थकारं ब्रह्मणो ज्ञेयं
दुर्गाबीजं दकारं स्याच्छ्यामं सर्वार्थसिद्धिदम् ३९

39. takāraṁ vāstu-daivatyaṁ śvetaṁ
thakāraṁ brahmaṇo jñeyaṁ
durgā-bījaṁ dakāraṁ syāc chyāmaṁ sarvārtha-siddhidam

धकारं धनदं प्रोक्तं पीताभं चार्थसिद्धिदम्
नकारं चैव सावित्री स्फाटिकं पापनाशनम् ४०

40. dhakāraṁ dhanadaṁ proktaṁ pītābhaṁ cārtha-siddhidam
nakāraṁ caiva sāvitrī sphāṭikaṁ pāpa-nāśanam

पकारं चैव पर्जन्यं शुक्लाभं वृष्टिसिद्धिदम्
फकारं पाशुपत्यं च सत्वः पापविनाशनम् ४१

41. pakāraṁ caiva parjanyaṁ śuklābhaṁ vṛṣṭi-siddhidam
phakāraṁ pāśupatyaṁ ca satvaḥ pāpa-vināśanam

बकारं तु त्रिमूर्तिः स्यात्पीतं सर्वार्थसिद्धिदम्
भकारं भार्गवं विन्द्याद्रक्तं भाग्यप्रदं भवेत् ४२

42. bakāraṁ tu tri-mūrtiḥ syāt pītaṁ sarvārtha-siddhidam
bhakāraṁ bhārgavaṁ vindyād raktaṁ bhāgya-pradaṁ bhavet

मकारं मदनं विन्द्याच्छ्यामं कामफलप्रदम्
यकारं वायुदैवत्यं कृष्णमुच्चाटनं भवेत् ४३

43. makāraṁ madanaṁ vindyāc chyāmaṁ kāma-phala-pradam
yakāraṁ vāyu-daivatyaṁ kṛṣṇam uccāṭanaṁ bhavet

रकारं वह्निदैवत्यं रक्ताभं राजसं भवेत्
लकारं पृथिवीबीजं पीतं स्यात् लम्भनं भवेत् ४४

44. rakāraṁ vahni-daivatyaṁ raktābhaṁ rājasaṁ bhavet
lakāraṁ pṛthivī-bījaṁ pītaṁ syāt lambhanaṁ bhavet

वकारं वारुणं बीजं शुक्लाभं योगनाशनम्
लक्ष्मीबीजं शकारं स्यात् हेमाभं राजसं भवेत् ४५

45. vakāraṁ vāruṇaṁ bījaṁ śuklābhaṁ yoga-nāśanam
lakṣmī-bījaṁ śakāraṁ syāt hemābhaṁ rājasaṁ bhavet

षकारं द्वादशात्मं स्यात् रक्ताभं तु जयप्रदम्
सकारं शक्तिबीजं स्याद्रक्तं स्थितिकरं भवेत् ४६

46. ṣakāraṁ dvādaśātmaṁ syāt raktābhaṁ tu jaya-pradam
sakāraṁ śakti-bījaṁ syād raktaṁ sthiti-karaṁ bhavet

हकारं शिवबीजं स्याच्छुद्धस्फटिकसन्निभम्
अणिमाद्यष्टसिद्धं च भुक्तिं मुक्तिं प्रयच्छति ४७

47. hakāraṁ śiva-bījaṁ syāc chuddha-sphaṭika-sannibham
aṇimādy-aṣṭa-siddhaṁ ca bhuktiṁ muktiṁ prayacchati

ळकारं चात्मबीजं स्याद्रक्ताभं सर्वसिद्धिदम् ४८

48. ḷakāraṁ cātma-bījaṁ syād raktābhaṁ sarva-siddhidam

इति वर्णशिक्षा समाप्ता

iti varṇa-śikṣā samāptā

Reference:
Descriptive Catalogue of Sanskrit Manuscripts in the Oriental Research Institute, University of Mysore. Mysore: Oriental Research Institute, Vol. II (Vedāṅgam, etc.), 1978. Catalogued as Varṇa-Liṅgādi-Nirṇaya, Manuscript Catalog entry #3756 (Palm Leaf Bundle #4772, Text #20 in that bundle). Palm Leaves, Telugu script, 4 folios, incomplete.

वर्णशिक्षा

वर्णानां स्त्रीपुंनपुंसकसंज्ञा

ककारं च गकारं च
चकारं च जकारकम्
टकारं च डकारं च
तकारं च दकारकम् १
पकारं च बकारं च
षकारं च क्षकारकम्
एते द्वादशवर्णाः स्युः
पुंल्लिङ्गाश्चेति कीर्तिताः २
खकारं च घकारं च
छकारं च झकारकम्
ठकारं च ढकारं च

थकारं च धकारकम् ३
फकारं च भकारं च
शकारं च सकारकम्
एते वै भानुबीजानि
जायाश्चेति प्रकीर्तिताः ४
शेषं नपुंसकं ज्ञेयं
त्रयो भेदा इति स्मृताः ५
शिवाग्निभूतरुद्राश्च
त्रयोदश तिथिस्तथा
एते वै स्वरवर्णाः स्युः
पुंल्लिङ्गाश्चेति कीर्तिताः ६
पक्षो वेदरसा भानुर्
मनुशैवाधिकारकाः
एतानि स्वरवर्णानि

स्त्रीलिङ्गानीति कीर्त्यते ७
प्रकृतिः सप्तवर्णानि
विकृतिस्तु नवार्णकम्
प्रकृतिर्ह्रस्वमित्युक्तं
विकृतिर्दीर्घमुच्यते ८
प्रथमाश्च तृतीयाश्च
षकारश्च क्षकारकम्
एते द्वादशवर्णाः स्युः
पुंल्लिङ्गाश्चेति कीर्तिताः ९
द्वितीयाश्च चतुर्थाश्च
शसकारौ तथैव च
एते द्वादशवर्णाः स्युः
स्त्रीलिङ्गाश्चेति प्रकीर्तिताः १०
अन्तस्थाश्चोत्तमाश्चैव

ॠ ॡ वर्णौ तथैव च
हकारश्च ळकारश्च
क्लीबाश्चेति प्रकीर्तिताः ११

वर्णानां सत्वरजस्तमो गुणाः
पक्षो गृहार्थसंख्या च
त्रयोदशमनुस्तथा
एते वै सात्विकगुणाः
श्वेतवर्णं तथैव च १२
शिवाब्धिसप्तावसुदिक्च
रुद्राः तिथिश्चैव कलास्तथा
एते वै राजसगुणा
रक्तवर्णं तथैव च १३
बाणो रसस्तृतीया च

श्यामवर्णा तमो गुणाः
हल्
द्वितीया च चतुर्थश्च
तवर्गप्रथमोत्तमौ १४
पवर्गप्रथमश्चैव
वेदाष्टादश एव च
एते वै सात्त्विकगुणाः
श्वेतवर्णा तथैव च १५
खकारं च घकारं च
ठकारं च थकारकम्
तकारं च नकारं च
पकारं च फकारकम्
वकारं च हकारश्च
क्षकारं चेति सात्त्विकः १६

कवर्गप्रथमश्चैव
टवर्गश्च तथैव च
तृतीयाश्च तपवर्गचतुर्थाश्च
चटवर्गोत्तमौ तथा १७
ऊष्माणश्चैव रेफश्च
लळकारौ रजोगुणाः
कवर्गप्रथमश्चैव
टवर्गश्च तथैव च १८
तृतीयाश्च भकारश्च
धकारं च ञकारकम्
णकारं चोष्मणश्चैव
रेफश्चैव लळौ तथा
एते रजोगुणाः प्रोक्ता
रक्तवर्णां तथैव च १९

चकारश्च द्वितीया च
ङकारं च मकारकम् २०
ढकारं च दकारं च
यकारं च झकारकम्
तामसः कृष्णवर्णा च
उत्तमश्च मिश्रकम् २१
चकारश्च द्वितीया च
आद्यन्तौ वर्गपञ्चमौ
चटवर्गचतुर्थौ च
तवर्गश्च तृतीयकम् २२
यकारस्तामसगुणः
श्यामवर्णास्तथैव च २३

अकारं सर्वदैवत्यं
रक्तवर्णं रजः स्मृतम्
आकारः स्यात्पराशक्तिः
श्वेतं सात्त्विकमुच्यते २४
इकारं विष्णुदैवत्यं
श्यामं तामसमुच्यते
मायाशक्तिरितीकारं
पीतं राजसमुच्यते २५
उकारं वास्तुदैवत्यं
कृष्णं तामसमीरितम्
ऊकारं भूमिदैवत्यं
श्यामळं तामसं भवेत् २६
ऋकारं ब्रह्मणो ज्ञेयं
पीतं राजसमुच्यते

शिखरिण्डरूपं ॠकारं
राजसं पीतवर्णकम् २७
अश्विनौ तु ऌ ॡ प्रोक्तौ
एकारं वीरभद्रं स्याद्
रजः पीतं तु सिद्धिदम् २८
ऐकारं वाग्भवं विन्द्यात्
ओकारमीश्वरं विन्द्याज्
ज्योतिः सत्वं फलप्रदम् २९
औकारमादिशक्तिः स्याच्
छुक्लं सर्वत्र सिद्धिदम्
अंकारं तु महेशं स्याद्
रक्तवर्णं तु राजसम् ३०
अःकारं कालरुद्रं च
रक्तं राजसमुच्यते

प्राजापत्यं ककारं स्यात्
पीतं वृष्टिप्रदं रजः ३१
खकारं जाह्नवीबीजं
क्षीराभं पापनाशनम्
गाणपत्यं गकारं स्याद्
रक्ताभं विघ्ननाशनम् ३२
घकारं भैरवं ज्ञेयं
मुक्ताभं शत्रुनाशनम्
ङकारं कालबीजं स्यात्
कालं तार्क्ष्यं समुच्यते ३३
चकारं चण्डरुद्रं स्यात्
अञ्जनाभं तु तामसम्
छकारं भद्रकाळी स्यात्
तामसं परिकीर्तितम् ३४

जकारं जम्भहा ज्ञेयं
रक्ताभं च जयावहम्
झकारमर्धनारीशं
श्यामरक्तं तु मिश्रकम् ३५
ञकारं सर्पदैवत्यं
पीतं राजसरूपकम्
भृङ्गीशं स्याट्टकारं तु
रक्तं राजसमेव च ३६
ठकारं चन्द्रबीजं स्याच्
छ्वेतं सात्त्विकमुच्यते
डकारं चैकनेत्रं स्यात्
पीतं राजसमुच्यते ३७
ढकारं यमबीजं स्यान्
नीलं मृत्युविनाशनम्

णकारं नन्दिबीजं स्याद्
रक्ताभं चार्थसिद्धिदम् ३८
तकारं वास्तुदैवत्यं श्वेतं
थकारं ब्रह्मणो ज्ञेयं
दुर्गाबीजं दकारं स्याच्
छ्यामं सर्वार्थसिद्धिदम् ३९
धकारं धनदं प्रोक्तं
पीताभं चार्थसिद्धिदम्
नकारं चैव सावित्री
स्फाटिकं पापनाशनम् ४०
पकारं चैव पर्जन्यं
शुक्लाभं वृष्टिसिद्धिदम्
फकारं पाशुपत्यं च
सत्वः पापविनाशनम् ४१

बकारं तु त्रिमूर्तिः स्यात्
पीतं सर्वार्थसिद्धिदम्
भकारं भार्गवं विन्द्याद्
रक्तं भाग्यप्रदं भवेत् ४२
मकारं मदनं विन्द्याच्
छ्यामं कामफलप्रदम्
यकारं वायुदैवत्यं
कृष्णामुच्चाटनं भवेत् ४३
रकारं वह्निदैवत्यं
रक्ताभं राजसं भवेत्
लकारं पृथिवीबीजं
पीतं स्यात् लम्भनं भवेत् ४४
वकारं वारुणं बीजं
शुक्लाभं योगनाशनम्

लक्ष्मीबीजं शकारं स्यात्
हेमाभं राजसं भवेत् ४५
षकारं द्वादशात्मं स्यात्
रक्ताभं तु जयप्रदम्
सकारं शक्तिबीजं स्याद्
रक्तं स्थितिकरं भवेत् ४६
हकारं शिवबीजं स्याच्
छुद्धस्फटिकसन्निभम्
अणिमाद्यष्टसिद्धं च
भुक्तिं मुक्तिं प्रयच्छति ४७
ळकारं चात्मबीजं स्याद्
रक्ताभं सर्वसिद्धिदम् ४८

इति वर्णशिक्षा समाप्ता

A Vision of the Complete Science of Śikṣā

According to *Śikṣādivedāṅgasūcī*, there are broadly three categories of texts that belong to the field of Śikṣā. We will call these "Śikṣā," "Upa-Śikṣā," and "Lakṣaṇa" texts.

1. **Śikṣā**: First are the textbooks which systematically present the theories of Sanskrit phonetics, including the alphabet, the rules of pronunciation, and the procedures for reciting the Vedic texts. These texts bear the names of the great seers of ancient times, the Śikṣākāras who wrote them. Śikṣādivedāṅgasūcī lists 18 seers, mostly associated with Kṛṣṇa Yajur Veda (see below, page 122). Currently we have 22 major treatises, named for their respective seers, representing all the four Vedas.

Major Phonetic Treatises

General:
1. Pāṇinīya Śikṣā
2. Āpiśali Śikṣā

Ṛg Veda:
3. Śaiśirīya Śikṣā
4. Śaunaka Śikṣā

Sāma Veda:
5. Nāradīya Śikṣā
6. Gautama Śikṣā
7. Lomaśī Śikṣā

Kṛṣṇa Yajur Veda:
8. Ātreya Śikṣā
9. Vyāsa Śikṣā
10. Śambhu Śikṣā
11. Vasiṣṭhī Śikṣā (2)
12. Kauṇḍinya Śikṣā (2)
13. Bhāradvāja Śikṣā
14. Pāri Śikṣā
15. Kauhalīya Śikṣā
16. Cārāyanīya Śikṣā
17. Vararuci Śikṣā

Śukla Yajur Veda
18. Amareśa Śikṣā
19. Amoghānandinī Śikṣā (2)
20. Yājñavalkya Śikṣā
21. Kauśikī Śikṣā

Atharva Veda
22. Māṇḍūkī Śikṣā

2. **Upa-Śikṣā:** Second is a broad class of texts dealing with specific issues of pronunciation and recitation. The Śikṣādivedāṅgasūcī lists 36 such texts. Here we include a number of different sets of texts: A) Texts named after great seers, which due to brevity, or narrow focus, didn't qualify for our list of *Śikṣā* texts; B) Comprehensive phonetic treatises with unnamed authors; C) Texts called Śikṣā that are narrowly addressing specific topics and issues; D) Texts not identified as "Śikṣā" which systematically address themes and topics that are important and relevant to Sanskrit phonetics; E) The Baiṭh literature, devoted to counting; F) The commentaries on Kṛṣṇa Yajur Veda Prātiśākhya. Most of these 36 Upaśikṣā texts listed in Śikṣādivedāṅgasūcī deal with topics from the Taittirīya recension of Kṛṣṇa Yajur Veda, so a comprehensive list including parallel texts from all the different Vedas might number nearly 200. Here we present about 90 different texts, dominated by the specialized texts belonging to the Taittirīya recension of Kṛṣṇa Yajur Veda.

Minor Phonetic Treatises

A. Texts Named After Great Seers

23. Ātreya Śikṣā (Madras)
24. Ātreya Śikṣā (Hoshiarpur)
25. Hayagrīvī Śikṣā
26. Kānva Śikṣā
27. Kātyāyana Śikṣā
28. Kātyāyanī Śikṣā (Bombay)
29. Keśavīya Śikṣā
30. Keśavī_padyātmikā Śikṣā
31. Laghumādhyandinīya Śikṣā
32. Laghvamoghānandinī Śikṣā
33. Lakṣmīkānta Śikṣā
34. Lakṣmīkānta Śikṣā (2)
35. Laugākṣi Śikṣā

36. Mādhyandinīya Śikṣā
37. Māṇḍavya Śikṣā
38. Pārāsharīya Śikṣā
39. Vāsiṣṭha Śikṣā (Adayar)
40. Vāsiṣṭha Śikṣā (Saṁgraha)
41. Vyāla Śikṣā
42. Vyāli Śikṣā (Aṣṭavikṛtivivṛtiḥ)
43. Vyāli Śikṣā

B. Comprehensive Phonetic Treatises

44. Sarvasaṁmata Śikṣā
45. Sarvasaṁmata Śikṣā Vyākhyā
46. Siddhānta Śikṣā
47. Śikṣāsamuccaya
48. Veda Śikṣā
49. Yājuṣabhūṣā commentary on Pāri Śikṣā

C. Narrowly focused Śikṣā

50. Avasānanirṇaya Śikṣā
51. Āruṇa Śikṣā
52. Galadṛk Śikṣā
53. Kālanirṇaya Śikṣā
54. Kramakārikā Śikṣā
55. Kramasaṁdhāna Śikṣā
56. Manaḥsvāra Śikṣā
57. Pluta Śikṣā
58. Prātiśākhyapradīpa Śikṣā
59. Ṣoḍaśaślokī Śikṣā
60. Svarabhaktilakṣaṇapariśiṣṭa Śikṣā
61. Svarasārabhūtavarṇakrama Śikṣā
62. Svara Śikṣā
63. Svaravyañjana Śikṣā

64. Svarāṅkuśa Śikṣā
65. Svarāṣṭaka Śikṣā
66. Varṇa Śikṣā
67. Vedaparibhāṣākārikā Śikṣā
68. Vedaparibhāṣāsūtra Śikṣā
69. Yajurvidhāna Śikṣā
70. Yohiprāpti Śikṣā

D. Phonetic Texts not named "Śikṣā"

71. Antanirdeśa
72. Atharvavediya Dantyoṣṭavidhi
73. Dvitva Lakṣaṇam
74. Hrasva Saṁgraha
75. Jaṭā Lakṣaṇam
76. Jaṭā Paṭala Kārikā
77. Jaṭāvali
78. Jaṭāvallī
79. Jaṭāmaṇi
80. Jaṭāmaṇi-vyākhyāna
81. Padacandrikā
82. Padakārikāratnamālā
83. Piṇḍalakṣaṇam
84. Praṇava Vicāra
85. Pratijñā Sūtram
86. Ṣaḍviṁśati sūtra
87. Svara Pañcāśat
88. Svarasamparki Savyākhyāna
89. Svarasārabhūtavarṇakrama Darpaṇa
90. Svarāṣṭaka
91. Svarāvadhānalakṣaṇa
92. Trikrama Lakṣaṇam
93. Tṛtīya Saṁgraha

94. Uccasvaranirṇaya
95. Uccodarki
96. Uccodarki Lakṣaṇa Vyākhyā
97. Varṇakramalakṣaṇa
98. Visargāṅgulipradarśanaprakāraḥ
99. Visarjanīya Lakṣaṇam
100. Yamāpatti
101. Yohi Bhāṣya of Sūribhaṭṭa

E. THE BAIṬH LITERATURE

103. Rāvaṇabaiṭh
104. Rāvaṇabaiṭh Paribhāṣā
105. Nāradabaiṭh
106. Nāradabaiṭh Vyākhyā
107. Vaidyanātha Baiṭh
108. Iṅgya Ratnam

F. COMMENTARIES ON KṚṢṆA YAJUR VEDA PRĀTIŚĀKHYA

109. Taittirīya Prātiśākhya
110. Māhiṣeya Bhāṣya of Taittirīya Prātiśākhya
111. Tribhāṣyaratna
112. Vaidikābharaṇa

3. **Lakṣaṇa:** The third category comprises a group of texts very closely tied to their corresponding Saṁhitās. These texts list the instances of specific phonetic events in the recitation of Saṁhitā. There are seven of these types of events, and so there are seven Lakṣaṇa for each Veda. We include in this category all the Śamāna literature, and also the Sarvānukramaṇikā, the texts which list the Ṛṣi, Devatā and Chandas for each Veda.

LAKṢAṆA

SAPTA LAKṢAṆA OF ṚG VEDA

113. Śamāna Śikṣā
114. Akhaṇḍa Mañjarī (Aniṅgya Lakṣaṇam) of Śeṣa Nārāyaṇa
115. Ṛgvilaṅghya of Nāgadeva
116. Avarṇi-Dīpa of Dakṣiṇāmūrti of Śrivatsagotra
117. Āvarṇi Prakaraṇam
118. Natānta-Padāni of Śeṣa Nārāyaṇa
119. Tapara Prakaraṇam of Śeṣa Nārāyaṇa

SAPTA LAKṢAṆA OF SĀMA VEDA

120. Śamāna
121. Visargalopa
122. Raṅga
123. Vilaṅghya
124. Ṇapara
125. Ṫapara
126. Avarṇi
127. Anavagraha

SAPTA LAKṢAṆA OF KṚṢṆA YAJUR VEDA

128. Śamāna
129. Vilaṅghya
130. Napara
131. Tapara
132. Avarṇi
133. Āvarṇi
134. Aniṅgya
135. Aniṅgya Śataka
136. Aniṅgya Grantha

ADDITIONAL LAKṢAṆA TEXTS

137. Āruṇa Śamānam
138. Śākhā Śamānam

SARVĀNUKRAMAṆIKĀ

139. Ṛg Veda Sarvānukramaṇikā
140. Sāma Veda Sarvānukramaṇikā
141. Śukla Yajur Veda Sarvānukramaṇikā
142. Kandānukramaṇika of Rishi Āpastamba
143. Atharva Veda Sarvānukramaṇikā

SUMMARY AND CONCLUSION

Dr. Tony Nader, M.D., Ph.D., in his book *Human Physiology, Expression of Veda and Vedic Literature* correlates Śikṣā with the 36 pairs of autonomic ganglia arranged along the spine. Here, in this Appendix, we have surveyed the entire literature of Śikṣā, and found that texts fit into three broad categories: 1) The texts of the Ṛsis, each of which presents a comprehensive overall view of the principles and practice of expression of the ancient Vedic language; 2) Topical texts, dealing with specific laws functioning within specific domains of expression, which we could call the Devatā or "organizing power" aspect of expression, and 3) Texts which connect principles of pronunciation to their actual listed occurrences in the Vedic Saṁhitā, which we call the specific, or Chandas aspect of expression. These three sub-groups or categories of knowledge together comprise the wholeness of knowledge of Śikṣā in the same way that the Vedic Saṁhitā itself is made up of streams of Ṛṣi, Devatā, and Chandas. If the comprehensive Vedic knowledge of Śikṣā is to be meaningfully correlated with the 36 pairs of autonomic ganglia, then it must be the case that all three categories of Śikṣā text are lively in that aspect of the physiology which supports the *expressing quality* of intelligence. There should be three Śikṣā texts, one Ṛṣi, one Devatā, and one Chandas, correlated with each of the 36 pairs of autonomic ganglia. This expands the range of texts to be included in the curriculum of Śikṣā to at least 108, while at the same time upholding and strengthening the correlation between Vedic Literature and the human physiology as described by Dr. Tony Nader.

Although currently only a fraction of the 143 Śikṣā texts listed here are in print, nearly all of them are available for study in Devanāgarī, online at http://www.peterffreund.com/shiksha/shiksha.html.

शिक्षादिवेदाङ्गसूची
ŚIKṢĀDI-VEDĀṄGA-SŪCĪ

भारद्वाजव्यासपारिशंभुकौहलहारिताः

बोधायनो वसिष्ठश्च वाल्मीकिश्च महामुनिः १

1. Bhāradvāja, Vyāsa, Pāri, Śambhu, Kauhala, Hārita, Bodhāyana, Vasiṣṭha, and the great sage Vālmīki—

अथापिशलिकौण्डिन्यपाणिन्यात्रेयनारदाः

पुलस्त्यबाडभीकारप्लाक्षिप्लाक्षायणास्तथा २

2. Now Āpiśali, Kauṇḍinya, Pāṇini, Ātreya, Nārada, Pulastya, Bāḍabhīkāra, Plākṣi, Plākṣāyaṇa, similarly—

मुनयोऽष्टादश ह्येते शिक्षाकाराः प्रकीर्तिताः

कालनिर्णयसिद्धान्तलक्ष्मीकान्तारुणास्तथा ३

3. These 18 sages are renowned as writers of Śikṣās. Similarly Kālanirṇaya, Siddhānta, Lakṣmīkānta, and Āruṇa—

सर्वसंमतशिक्षा च स्याच्छिक्षाचन्द्रिका ततः

माहिषेयकारिका च तथा शिक्षासमुच्चयः ४

4. And Sarvasaṁmata Śikṣā should be included, and further Śikṣā Candrikā. Further Māhiṣeya Kārikā, and similarly Śikṣā Samuccaya.

उच्चोदर्कि वैद्यनाथबैड् जटाचन्द्रिका अपि

जटावलिर्योहिभाष्यं सा जटामणिरित्यपि ५

5. Moreover, Uccodarki, Vaidyanāthabaiṭ, Jaṭā Candrikā, Jaṭāvali, Yohi Bhāṣya and that jewel Jaṭāmaṇi—

स्यात्प्रातिशाख्यमात्रेयभाष्यं वररुचेरपि

स्यान्माहिषेयभाष्यं च तथा तत्सूत्रकारिका ६

6. The (Taittirīya) Prātiśākhya, and the commentaries of Ātreya, Vararuci, Māhiṣeya, and similarly the Sūtra Kārikā—

ततस्त्रिभाष्यरत्नं च वैदिकाभरणं तथा

दीपं याजुषभूषा च स्याद्वर्णक्रमदर्पणम् ७

7. Further, the Tribhāṣya Ratna, the Vaidikābharaṇa, the Dīpa and the Yājuṣabhūṣā (commentaries) should be included, and the Varṇakrama Darpaṇa.

अथ शिक्षासंग्रहश्च स्याद्वर्णसारदीपिका

तथैव स्वरपञ्चाशत् स्वरावधानदर्पणम् ८

8. Now Śikṣā Saṁgraha and Varṇasāradīpikā should be included, and similarly Svarapañcāśat and Svarāvadhāna Darpaṇa.

स्वरचूडामणिश्चान्तनिर्देशः सप्तलक्षणम्

वर्णक्रमचतुःश्लोकी तथा रावणबैडपि ९

9. Svaracūḍāmaṇi and Antanirdeśa, Saptalakṣaṇa, Varṇakrama, and Catuḥślokī, and Rāvaṇa Baiṭ similarly—

स्यात् षड्विंशतिसूत्रं च योहिप्राप्तिस्तथैव च

१०

10. Should be included, and Ṣaḍviṁśati Sūtra and Yohi Prāpti similarly.

इति शिक्षादिवेदाङ्गसूची समाप्ता

Thus ends the table of contents (Śikṣādivedāṅgasūcī) of the first Vedāṅga, called "Śikṣā."

The Sanskrit Alphabet: Meeting Point Between Individuality and Universality
Maharishi Mahesh Yogi, 2 February 2005

The individual like a point, and cosmos like infinity—individual like a drop, and cosmos like the ocean—Where is the connection of the point with the ocean? Listen carefully: Where is the connecting point between the individual and the ocean? It is in the physiology of everyone. [It is in] that part of the physiology which pulsates in order to produce a syllable "a."

"a" is the syllable which expresses Ātmā, "a—tmā.[1] So "a" is the syllable expressing Ātmā. Now this is one thing.

---

1 Maharishi explains that two "a"s together, "a", "a", or "ā" represent continuum of "a," infinity. ("t" is a letter affixed to a vowel in grammatical shorthand notation, to point to that letter, to name that letter); "ma" he explains as the point of infinity: The Self is from "a" to "ma," from infinity to its own point. In the Self, in the Ātmā, the whole enormous, unbounded field of dynamism of Natural Law is there, humming within a point. So the Self, the Ātmā is like the point of a lens: Through a point in the lens you see the whole panorama on the other side, that means through a point you comprehend the whole enormous unbounded field of Cosmic Law, and that is the Self, that is Ātmā. (From Maharishi's Press Conference April 9, 2003).

Second thing is: "a" is the first syllable of the Veda. Veda is the Total Natural Law. Veda, the total Veda, whatever is the spread of Veda, it has its starting point in "a." *Agnim īḷe purohitam*: This is the beginning of the Veda—"a." So "a" is the first syllable of the Veda. That means "a" is the fountainhead of the flow of Veda. So "a" for Ātmā; "a"—the sound expressing Ātmā; and "a," the sound expressing Total Knowledge.

Total Knowledge is on two levels in "a": one is the sound of "a," which is the flow, and the other is inside the flow, which is eternal silence, which is Ātmā. Ātmā is expressed by a flow, but it is nonexpressed in a nonflow, in the silent value. So it is the "a" that is the meeting point of the individual and cosmic.

Now in the physiology, "a" has a place. In the physiology—this we know from the Vedic literature:[2] how "a" comes to be. "a" comes to be by the pulsation of

2 Maharishi is referring to the description of the origin and generation of speech sounds in Pāṇinīya Śikṣā, v.6-7: Ātmā buddhyā sametyārthān mano yuṅkte vivakṣayā, manaḥ kāyāgnimāhanti sa prerayati mārutam, mārutas tūrasi caran mandraṁ janayati svaram. The Self stirs with an intention. Together with the intellect, it takes a direction, and engages the mind. The mind strikes the fire of the body, which in turn drives out the air. The air, moving within the lungs, causes the emergence of subtle sound, which becomes sound—svaram: The reverberation of the Self.

that part of the throat—physiology. Throat is a hollow something—hollow. But that hollow is just like the hollowness of the seed.[3] But the hollowness pulsates. And when the hollowness pulsates, then it is the pulsation of the unmanifest. It is the pulsation of the unmanifest. So when unmanifest pulsates, it's the totality that pulsates—infinity, unboundedness, that pulsates. That means there is a time—we can now just imagine it in terms of time—there is a time when infinity is silent, and now there is a time when infinity pulsates. There is a time when the throat is all silent, and there is a time when the throat pulsates to produce "a." So this pulsation of the silence, the pulsation of the silence producing the sound "a," is a connection between the individuality and cosmic reality.

Constitution of the Universe—the Constitution of the Universe, Natural Law, Total Natural Law—is lively on that level where the physiology of the throat, the emptiness of the throat, pulsates in the syllable "a." So

3 Story from the Upanishads: The teacher asks the student to bring the fruit of the banyan tree. He brings it. "Now open it." The student opens the fruit. "What do you see?" The student replies, "Many seeds." The teacher says, "Take one seed and break it." The student breaks it. "What do you see?" The student says, "It's hollow inside." The teacher explains that from that hollowness, the whole great huge enormously diverse banyan tree comes up.

here is the meeting point of the Cosmic Constitution of the Universe in order to create the individual laws of nature which will control the individual activity. So in the throat, there is that hollowness, which is full of what? [It is] Full of memory. And full of memory is that one syllable "a"—"a." When we go into "a,"[4] then "a," "i," "u"—all these vowels and consonants of the Vedic literature—they all emerge from this one-syllable Constitution of the Universe, which is "a."

So there on the throat—hollowness of the throat—there on the hollowness of the throat, in an area of physiology, is the connecting switch for individual and the potential cosmic reality within the individual. So all the variety of the individual is concentrated, so to say, is unified, in that one little syllable "a." And the reverberation of that empty hollowness of the throat is a connecting link between the enormous cosmic dynamism of the cosmos, of the universe, and the inner silence of the individual and the inner faintest impulse: [the] first "a."

In the Vedic language, there is an expression about

4 When we go into "a" refers to the analysis of "a" in terms of eight levels of expression unfolded in the eight somersaults as "a" collapses into the silence of "ka." In these eight somersaults, all the vowels and all the consonants are created.

"a": *akāro [vai] sarvā vāk.*[5] Three words, only three words: akāro sarvā vāk. 'A' is the total speech," that's all. "a" is the total speech. This, on the level of speech, is [the] sound "a," but on the level of physiology, it's the throat—and in [the] throat, [it is the] hollowness of the throat. Here is a level which connects the individual with his cosmic potential.

Individual desire and cosmic desire: What is cosmic desire? Cosmic desire [is seen] pulsating—[in the] pulsating universe, back and forth, in and out and in and out—both ways, in and out, in and out. In both ways, in and out, is the whole story about the character of the Constitution of the Universe, which is fully awake within the syllable "a." And in the syllable "a," there is "i," and there is "u"—the whole story is there. It's a very beautiful field of knowledge. ...

Cosmic Constitution, total field of knowledge and action, is Veda. And that is abstractly in Ātmā, and that is concretely in the pulsating throat. So all these consonants and vowels of the Vedic language, they constitute the language of the Constitution of the Universe. So the whole Constitution of the Universe is there within the physiology and within the specific fluctuations of the physiology—[the] throat, the palate, the lips, [and]

5 Aitareya Āraṇyaka 2.3.6.

the tongue. Different, different areas are there which are responsible for the vowels and consonants of the Total Knowledge. And this is a natural thing.

This is a natural thing. This is not a thing of learning on "a." The boy is born with "a," [and then there is a] relationship of the child and the mother [in] "a": the child says, "a"; the mother says, "a." These are the surface levels of explanation—just amusements. But the reality is that the individual has the switchboard within his physiology. That is like the press button operation of a computer: Only that thing will reverberate. You press the button, and that thing will reverberate. And how that thing is related to other things? In a sequential manner. Very important is the word "sequential"—sequential. From "a" to "i" to "u" to "ṛ" to "e," "ai," "o," "au," "aṁ," "aḥ"—this whole alphabet, the sequential evolution of it, all the vowels and consonants in sequence—this is just the sequence of the emptiness of the seed: [first there is the] emptiness within the seed, and then the seed becoming lively and pulsating, and then sprouting [starts], and the sprouting becomes bigger and bigger, and becomes plant and tree and huge, big tree, infinite variety of the leaves and branches and all that. Exactly like a tree and its relation with the unmanifest seed [is the sequential expansion of speech from "a"]. . . . .

EPILOG 130

This is the field of creation. [It is] realistic and practical and absolutely simple, because that is the nature of the individual life and cosmic life. The meeting point of the individuality and cosmic reality, [is the] meeting point of individual law [with cosmic law]. [In the individual desire and action] which means this desire, this desire, this action, this action—the cosmic law works silently, silently. . . . All these different fields of knowledge—chemistry, physics, or whatever—we may say different religions, or whatever—they are all embedded on this level, where the Cosmic Constitution meets with the individual performance: Just that area of the throat, that area of the palate, that area of the [physiology] from where all these letters come out.

The letters form in a systematic way. In a sequential manner, [the letters] form the words, and the words form the combination of words, and they form sentences, and the sentences form the paragraphs, and paragraphs form the chapters, and chapters form the whole book. Sequentially evolving, sequentially evolving—But the starting point of this evolution is on that level where the individuality and the cosmic reality are both on the junction point. They are both meeting, like a lamp at the door: Like a lamp at the door.

Index

A

"a"
  all the devatās 20, 31, 45
  collapse of "a" 3
  first vowel 18
  letter 5, 18
  part of every letter 20, 30
Abdhi 33
Ādiśakti 47, 60
administration of the universe 22
Agni 76
akāro vai sarvā vāk 129
Akṣara 5
alliterative devatās 82
alphabet 7, 27, 35, 115
aṇimā 52
Āpiśali Śikṣā 7
Ardhanārīśa 49, 65
Artha 33
Aśvins 47, 58
Ātmā 53, 79, 81, 125, 129
Ātreya 59
Ātreya Śikṣā 7, 8
autonomic ganglia 2, 121, 122

B

Bāṇa 33
bestowing all powers 53
bestowing good fortune 51
bestowing victory 52
bestows siddhis 47, 53
Bhadrakālī 48, 64
Bhairava 48, 63
Bhānu 33
Bhārgava 51, 73
Bhṛṅgīśa 49, 66
bhukti 53
Bhūmi 46, 56, 57
binding the boundless 28
boons 23, 27, 87-90
Brahman 4, 30, 46, 50, 57, 69
bringing victory 49

C

Caṇḍarudra 48, 64
Candra 66
ca-varga 44, 45
chandas 17
city of the gods 16
cognition 17, 25
collapse of "a" to "ka" 3, 5, 6, 19
colophon 26
color 31, 42
color of letters 15, 23, 27, 54
completeness of Varṇa Śikṣā 27
conveyances 51, 76
Cosmic Constitution 131
Cosmic desire 129
creating stability 52

D

Dakṣa 59
Dasra 58
destroying boundaries 52
destroying death 50
destroying enemies 24, 51
destroying evil 24, 51
destroying obstacles 48
Devanāgarī 16
devatā 16, 19, 21, 23, 27, 121
Devatās, Colors, and Qualities 45
Devī 76
Dhanada 69
Dhanvantari 59
Digambara 63
Dik 33
Divine Being 24
Divine Mothers 64
Durgā 50, 60, 64, 69
Dvādaśātmā 79

E

earth 4, 76
Earth devatā 46
earth element 51
ego 4
eight elements 4
eight somersaults 3, 52
Ekanetra 67
enemy-destroying 48
enlightenment 4
eternal bliss consciousness, XI
eternal silence 126
expression 1, 7, 10
expression of the infinite 30

F

feminine 13, 39
First Science 20
flow of natural law 32
flow of speech 22
flow of wholeness 35
form 8
forty branches of Vedic Literature, XII, 38
fruit of desire 24, 51
fulfillment of every goal 50
fundamental organizing principles 23

G

Gaṇapati 48, 62
Gaṇeṣa 48, 62
Gaṅgā 61
garimā 53
Garuḍa 56
Gautama Śikṣā 7
gender of letters 11, 13, 27, 39
giving victory 24
god of love 51, 74

H

half-male-half-female 49, 65
hollowness of the throat 128
homeostatic balance 2
Human Physiology, Expression of Veda and Vedic Literature 2, 121
human speech 22

I

ideal education 35
imperishable 5
impulses of consciousness 4, 13
incarnations of Viṣṇu 55
Indian paleography 33
Indra 65
infinite consciousness 18, 30
infinite dynamism 12, 21
infinite potential of man 4
infinite silence 21
Iṅgya Ratnam 32
intellect 4
interdisciplinary study 20, 21
Īśa 65
Īśitva 53
Īśvara 60

J

Jāhnavī 48, 61
Jaimini 8, 9
Jambhahā 49, 65
Jñānaśakti 55
Josephson, Brian 15
Jyotir Liṅgas 72, 79

K

Kalā 33
Kāla 63
Kālarudra 47, 61
Kāmadeva 51, 74
kāra, letter 34
Karma Mīmāṁsā 8, 9
Kaṭapay system 32
ka-varga 43
Kriyāśakti 55
kshara of "a" 5
Kumareśa 63

L

laghimā 53
Lakṣmī 52, 56, 69, 78
lamp at the door 35, 131
language 32
Lord of Beginnings 62
lord of cattle 51
lore of Śikṣā 28

M

Madana 74
Madhucchandas level 12
Maheśa 47, 60
mahimā 53
Mahiṣāsura 69
Manu 33

Manuscript of Varṇa Śikṣā 9, 26 (including URL)
masculine 13, 39
mastery of all things 50
Māyā 60
Māyā Śakti 46, 56
meaning of Vedic words 10
Moon 49, 66
Mother Divine 83
Mother Gaṅgā 48
Mṛtsañjīvanī 59
mukti 53

N

name and form 8, 9, 10, 11, 23, 31, 34
Nandi 50, 68
nasals 41
Nāsatya 58
neuter 13, 39
number systems 32

O

one-eyed 49
one unbounded ocean of consciousness 31, 35
organizing principles 22
organizing power 7, 23, 30, 31, 35

P

paleography 33
palm leaves 26
Pañca Devatās 62
Parā 21
Parāśakti 45, 55
Parjanya 51, 70
Paśupati 51, 72
Patañjali 10
Pātañjali kaivalya 11
pa-varga 43
perfection in every area 47
perfection in rain 51
phalaśruti of letters 23
Pra-impulses 15
Prajāpati 48, 61
prākāmya 53
prāpti 53
Prakṛti 4, 5, 12, 40
primordial creative power 47
process of knowing 17
pronunciation 7
Pṛthivī 52, 62, 76
Pu-impulses 15
pure consciousness 20, 23, 30
Puruṣa 12
Puruṣa Sūkta 61, 66

Q

qualities of Vedic sounds 13

R

rain 24, 31, 51, 70
rain-bestowing 48

rajas 14, 23, 42, 44
rajasic letters 15
Ramā 56
Rāma 11
Rāma Charita Mānasa 11
Rāmāyaṇa 11
Rasa 33
Remover of Obstacles 62
removing obstacles 24
repelling death 24
repha 44
representing numbers with words 32
Ṛgveda 3, 55, 60
ṛcas 3, 4, 25
Ṛco akṣare 3
Ritaṁ Bharā Pragyā 10
Rudra 33, 73

S

Śaivādhikārakāḥ 33
Śakti 52, 80
Samādhi 11, 19, 21
Saṁhitā of Ṛṣi, Devatā and Chandas, XI, 121
Sanskrit alphabet 7, 20, 31
Sarasvatī 69
Sarpa 49, 66
sarvadaivatya 55
sattva 14, 23, 43
Sat-Cit-Ānanda, XI
sattva, rajas and tamas 27, 31
of letters 42
sattvic letters 15
Sāvitrī 50, 69
seers of the Vedāṅgas 25
Self-realization 6
self-referral 1, 2, 22
semi-vowels 7, 41
sequential emergence of sound 22, 25, 130
sequential evolution 10, 130
Śikṣā 6, 7, 115-124
sibilants 7, 14, 44
Śikhaṇḍin 46, 57
silence 11, 22
silence and dynamism 22, 31, 32
Śiva 52, 59, 60, 63, 66, 68, 72, 80
Skanda 64
snake devatā 49
sound and form 8, 10, 35
source of all creation 29
Śrilakṣmī 56
structuring dynamics of Ṛk Veda 1
structuring mechanics of creation 25
supreme knowledge 7
Svara 18

T

Taittirīya Saṁhitā 32

tamas 14, 23
tamasic letters 15
Tārkṣya 48
ta-varga 43, 44, 45
ṭa-varga 43, 44, 45
Telugu 8, 26
Time 48, 61, 63
total knowledge 6, 11, 30, 35, 55, 69, 126
total natural law 4, 31, 68, 126
transcendental consciousness 11, 19, 21
Trimūrti 51, 72
truth of Vedic sounds 10
twelve Jyotir Liṅgas 52
Twin Letters 82

U

Umā 65
unbounded wholeness 11, 18
Unmanifest Home of CI 12
Upanishads 30, 80

V

Vāgbhava 47, 60
Vahni 51, 76
Vāmana 61
varga 41
Varṇa-lingādi-nirṇaya 26, 100
Varṇa Śikṣa 5, 8, 118
Varuṇa 52, 78
Vāruṇa Purāṇa, 73
Vāstu devatā 46, 50, 56, 68
vaśitva 53
Vasu 33
Vāyu 51, 74
Vedas XI, 25
Vedic cognition 25
Vedic Literatuer, XII, 38
Vedic phonology 4, 21, 22, 36
Vedic system of education 10, 11
Vidyeśvaras 57, 67, 72, 73
vighna-nāśanam 48
vikṛti 40
Vīrabhadra 47, 59, 64
Viśalyakaraṇī 59
Viṣṇu 46, 55, 79
vital essence of speech 47

W

wealth bestowing 50
wholeness of life 30
words representing vowels 33

Y

Yama 50, 67
yamas 7
Yoga 10
Yoga Sūtra 10
yogic flying 53

Printed in Great Britain
by Amazon

69936374R00088